Multiple Intelligences

GRADE **3**

teaching kids the way they learn

written by
**Barbara G. Hoffman and
Kim Thoman**

Cover by Dawn Devries Sokol
Interior illustrations by Roberta Collier-Morales and Carol Faller
Symbol design by Rose Sheifer

FS-23282 Multiple Intelligences: Teaching Kids the Way They Learn Grade 3
All rights reserved. Printed in the U.S.A.
Copyright © 1999 Frank Schaffer Publications, Inc.
23740 Hawthorne Blvd., Torrance, CA 90505

TABLE of CONTENTS

What Is the Multiple Intelligences Theory?

The Multiple Intelligences Theory, developed and researched by Dr. Howard Gardner, recognizes the multifaceted profile of the human mind. In his book *Frames of Mind* (Basic Books, 1993) Dr. Gardner explains that every human possesses several intelligences in greater or lesser degrees. Each person is born with a unique intelligence profile and uses any or all of these intelligences to acquire knowledge and experience.

At present Gardner has defined eight intelligences. Below are the intelligences and a simplified definition of each. A more complete explanation of each intelligence is found at the end of the introduction.

- verbal-linguistic: word intelligence
- logical-mathematical: number and reasoning intelligence
- visual-spatial: picture intelligence
- musical-rhythmic: music and rhythm intelligence
- bodily-kinesthetic: body intelligence
- interpersonal: social intelligence
- intrapersonal: self intelligence
- naturalist: natural environment intelligence

Gardner stresses that although intelligence is a biological function, it is inseparable from the cultural context in which it exists. He cites the example of Bobby Fischer, the chess champion. In a culture without chess, Fischer would not have been able to become a good chess player.

The Multiple Intelligences Theory in the Classroom

The Multiple Intelligences Theory has been making its way into the educational setting over the past decade. Instinctively, educators have recognized that their students learn differently, respond uniquely to a variety of teaching techniques, and have their individual preferences. Traditional educational programs do not recognize the unique intelligence profile of each student. Traditionally educators have operated according to the belief that there is a single type of intelligence, based on a combination of math and verbal ability. This more one-dimensional view gave rise to the commonly held definition of an "IQ." According to this definition, all individuals are born with this general ability and it does not change with age, training, or experience. Dr. Gardner's theory plays a significant role in rethinking how to educate so as to meet each student's individual needs. Basic skills can be more effectively acquired if all of a student's strengths are involved in the learning process.

The key to lesson design for a multiple intelligences learning environment is to reflect on the concept you want to teach and identify the intelligences that seem most appropriate for communicating the content. At Mountlake Terrace High School in Edmonds, Washington, Eeva Reeder's math students learn about algebraic equations kinesthetically by using the pavement in the school's yard like a giant graph. Using the large, square cement blocks of the pavement, they identify the axes, the X and Y coordinates, and plot themselves as points on the axes.

Other teachers will attempt to engage all eight intelligences in their lessons by using learning centers to focus on different approaches to the same concept. An example of this is Bruce Campbell's third grade classroom in Marysville, Washington. Campbell, a consultant on teaching through multiple intelligences, has designed a unit on Planet Earth that includes seven centers: a building center where students use clay to make models of the earth; a math center; a reading center; a music center where students study unit spelling words while listening to music; an art center using concentric circle patterns; a cooperative learning activity; a writing center titled "Things I would take with me on a journey to the center of the earth."

Another way to use the multiple intelligences theory in the classroom is through student projects. For example, Barbara Hoffman had her third-grade students in Country Day School in Costa Rica develop games in small groups. The students had to determine the objective and rules of the game. They researched questions and answers and designed and assembled a game board and accessories. Many intelligences were engaged through the creation of this project.

Dr. Gardner recommends that schools personalize their programs by providing apprenticeships. These should be designed to allow students to pursue their interests, with an emphasis on acquiring expertise over a period of time. In the Escuela Internacional Valle del Sol in Costa Rica, apprenticeships based on the eight intelligences are used. In one program long-term special subjects are offered to students in areas such as cooking, soccer, and drama. In addition, at the end of the term the entire school participates in a special project in multiage grouping with activities focused around a theme such as Egypt or European medieval life.

Assessment

The multiple intelligences theory challenges us to redefine assessment and see it as an integral part of the learning process. Dr. Gardner believes that many of the intelligences do not lend themselves to being measured by standardized paper and pencil tests. In a classroom structured on the multiple intelligences theory, assessment is integrated with learning and instruction and stimulates further learning. The teacher, the student, and his or her peers are involved in ongoing assessment. In this way the student has a better understanding of his or her strengths and weaknesses. Self-evaluation gives students the opportunity to set goals, to use higher-order thinking skills, as well as to generalize and personalize what they learn.

One example of nontraditional assessment is the development and maintenance of student portfolios, including drafts, sketches, and final products. Both student and teacher choose pieces that illustrate the student's growth. (Gardner calls these *process folios*.) Self-assessment can also include parental assessment, as well as watching videotaped student performances, and students editing or reviewing each other's work.

How to Use This Book

Multiple Intelligences: Teaching Kids the Way They Learn Grade 3 is designed to assist teachers in implementing this theory across the curriculum. This book is for teachers of students in third grade. It is divided into six subject areas: language arts, social studies, mathematics, science, fine arts, and physical education. Each subject area offers a collection of practical, creative ideas for teaching each of the eight intelligences. The book also offers reproducible student worksheets to supplement many of these activities. (A small image of the worksheet can be found next to the activity it supplements. Answers are provided at the end of the book.) Teachers may pick and choose from the various activities to develop a multiple intelligences program that meets their students' needs.

The activities are designed to help the teacher engage all the intelligences during t[...]
that the unique qualities of each student are recognized, encouraged, and cultivated[...]
provide opportunities for students to explore their individual interests and talents while lea[...]
basic knowledge and skills that all must master. Each activity focuses on one intelligence; however, o[...]
intelligences will come into play since the intelligences naturally interact with each other.

As a teacher, you have the opportunity to provide a variety of educational experiences that can help students excel in their studies as well as discover new and exciting abilities and strengths within themselves. Your role in the learning process can provide students with an invaluable opportunity to fulfill their potential and enrich their lives.

Words of Advice

The following are some tips to assist you in using the Multiple Intelligences Theory in your classroom.

- Examine your own strengths and weaknesses in each of the intelligences. Call on others to help you expand your lessons to address the entire range of intelligences.

- Spend time in the early weeks of the school year working with your students to evaluate their comfort and proficiency within the various intelligences. Use your knowledge of their strengths to design and implement your teaching strategies.

- Refrain from "pigeonholing" your students into limited areas of intelligence. Realize that a student can grow from an activity that is not stressing his or her dominant intelligence.

- Work on goal-setting with students and help them develop plans to attain their goals.

- Develop a variety of assessment strategies and record-keeping tools.

- Flexibility is essential. The Multiple Intelligences Theory can be applied in a myriad of ways. There is no one right way.

e Eight Intelligences

Below is a brief definition of each of the eight intelligences, along with tips on how to recognize the characteristics of each and how to develop these intelligences in your students.

Verbal-Linguistic Intelligence

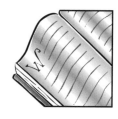

Verbal-linguistic intelligence consists of:

- a sensitivity to semantics—the meaning of words

- a sensitivity to syntax—the order among words

- a sensitivity to phonology—the sounds, rhythms, and inflections of words

- a sensitivity to the different functions of language, including its potential to excite, convince, stimulate, convey information, or please

Verbal-linguistic intelligence consists of the ability to think in words and to use words effectively, whether orally or in writing. The foundation of this intelligence is laid before birth, when the fetus develops hearing while still in the womb. It continues to develop after birth. Authors, poets, newscasters, journalists, public speakers, and playwrights are people who exhibit high degrees of linguistic intelligence.

People who are strongly linguistic like to read, write, tell stories or jokes, and play word games. They enjoy listening to stories or to people talking. They may have a good vocabulary or a good memory for names, places, dates, and trivia. They may spell words accurately and communicate to others effectively. They might also exhibit the ability to learn other languages.

Verbal-linguistic intelligence can be stimulated and developed in the classroom by providing a language rich environment. Classrooms in every subject area should include activities to help students develop a passion for language through speaking, hearing, reading, and examining words. Have students write stories, poems, jokes, letters, or journals. Provide opportunities for impromptu speaking, rapping, debate, storytelling, oral reading, silent reading, choral reading, and oral presentations. Involve students in class discussions and encourage them to ask questions and listen. Invite students to use storyboards, tape recorders, and word processors. Plan field trips to libraries, newspapers, or bookstores. Supply nontraditional materials such as comics and crossword puzzles to interest reluctant students.

Writing, listening, reading, and speaking effectively are key skills. The development of these four parts of linguistic intelligence can have a significant effect on a student's success in learning all subject areas and throughout life.

Logical-Mathematical Intelligence

Logical-mathematical intelligence consists of:

- the ability to use numbers effectively

- the ability to use inductive and deductive reasoning

- the ability to recognize abstract patterns

This intelligence encompasses three broad, interrelated fields: math, science, and logic. It begins when young children confront the physical objects of the world and ends with the understanding of abstract ideas. Throughout this process, a person develops a capacity to discern logical or numerical patterns and to handle long chains of reasoning. Scientists, mathematicians, computer programmers, bankers, accountants, and lawyers exhibit high degrees of logical-mathematical intelligence.

People with well-developed logical-mathematical intelligence like to find patterns and relationships among objects or numbers. They enjoy playing strategy games such as chess or checkers and solving riddles, logical puzzles, or brain teasers. They organize or categorize things and ask questions about how things work. These people easily solve math problems quickly in their heads. They may have a good sense of cause and effect and think on a more abstract or conceptual level.

Logical-mathematical intelligence can be stimulated and developed in the classroom by providing an environment in which students frequently experiment, classify, categorize, and analyze. Have students notice and work with numbers across the curriculum. Provide activities that focus on outlining, analogies, deciphering codes, or finding patterns and relationships.

Most adults use logical-mathematical intelligence in their daily lives to calculate household budgets, to make decisions, and to solve problems. Most professions depend in some way on this intelligence because it encompasses many kinds of thinking. The development of logical-mathematical intelligence benefits all aspects of life.

Bodily-Kinesthetic Intelligence

Bodily-kinesthetic intelligence consists of:

- the ability to control one's body movements to express ideas and feelings
- the capacity to handle objects skillfully, including the use of both fine and gross motor movements
- the ability to learn by movement, interaction, and participation

Bodily-kinesthetic intelligence begins with the control of automatic and voluntary movement and progresses to using the body in highly differentiated ways. The skillful manipulation of one's body or an object requires an acute sense of timing and direction, as well as the ability to transform an intention into action. Examples of people who possess bodily-kinesthetic intelligence are a dancer using his or her body as an object for expressive purposes and a basketball player who manipulates a ball with finesse. This intelligence can be seen in inventors, mechanics, actors, surgeons, swimmers, and artists.

People who are strongly bodily-kinesthetic enjoy working with their hands, have good coordination, and handle tools skillfully. They enjoy taking things apart and putting them back together. They prefer to manipulate objects to solve problems. They move, twitch, tap, or fidget while seated for a long time. They cleverly mimic other's gestures.

Many people find it difficult to understand and retain information that is taught only through their visual and auditory modes. They must manipulate or experience what they learn in order to understand and remember information. Bodily-kinesthetic individuals learn through doing and through multi-sensory experiences.

Bodily-kinesthetic intelligence can be stimulated and developed in the classroom through activities that involve physical movements such as role-playing, drama, mime, charades, dance, sports, and exercise. Have your students put on plays, puppet shows, or dance performances. Provide opportunities for students to manipulate and touch objects through activities such as painting, clay modeling, or building. Plan field trips to the theater, art museum, ballet, craft shows, and parks.

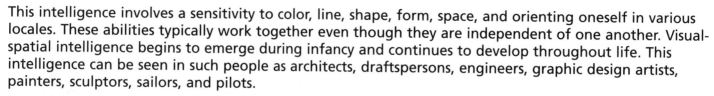

Visual-Spatial Intelligence

Visual-spatial intelligence consists of:

- the ability to perceive the visual-spatial world accurately
- the ability to think in pictures or visual imagery
- the ability to graphically represent visual or spatial ideas
- the ability to orient the body in space

This intelligence involves a sensitivity to color, line, shape, form, space, and orienting oneself in various locales. These abilities typically work together even though they are independent of one another. Visual-spatial intelligence begins to emerge during infancy and continues to develop throughout life. This intelligence can be seen in such people as architects, draftspersons, engineers, graphic design artists, painters, sculptors, sailors, and pilots.

Spatially skilled people enjoy art activities, jigsaw or visual perception puzzles, and mazes. They like to construct three-dimensional models. These people get more out of pictures than words in reading materials. They may excel at reading maps, charts, and diagrams. Also, they may have a good sense of direction.

Visual-spatial intelligence can be stimulated and developed in the classroom by providing a visually rich environment in which students frequently focus on images, pictures, and color. Provide opportunities for reading maps and charts, drawing diagrams and illustrations, constructing models, painting, coloring, and solving puzzles. Play games that require visual memory or spatial acuity. Use guided imagery, pretending, or active imagination exercises to have students solve problems. Use videos, slides, posters, charts, diagrams, telescopes, or color-coded material to teach the content area. Visit art museums, historical buildings, or planetariums.

Visual-spatial intelligence is an object-based intelligence. It functions in the concrete world, the world of objects and their locations. This intelligence underlies all human activity.

Musical Intelligence

Musical intelligence consists of:

- a sensitivity to pitch (melody), rhythm, and timbre (tone)
- an appreciation of musical expressiveness
- an ability to express oneself through music, rhythm, or dance

Dr. Gardner asserts that of all forms of intelligence, the consciousness-altering effect of musical intelligence is probably the greatest because of the impact of music on the state of the brain. He suggests that many individuals who have had frequent exposure to music can manipulate pitch, rhythm, and timbre to participate with some skill in composing, singing, or playing instruments. The early childhood years appear to be the most crucial period for musical growth. This intelligence can be seen in composers, conductors, instrumentalists, singers, and dancers.

Musically skilled people may remember the melodies of songs. They may have a good singing voice and tap rhythmically on a surface. Also, they may unconsciously hum to themselves and may be able to identify when musical notes are off-key. They enjoy singing songs, listening to music, playing an instrument, or attending musical performances.

Musical intelligence can be stimulated and developed in the classroom by providing opportunities to listen to musical recordings, to create and play musical instruments, or to sing and dance. Let students express their feelings or thoughts through using musical instruments, songs, or jingles. Play background music while the students are working. Plan field trips to the symphony, a recording studio, a musical, or an opera.

There are strong connections between music and emotions. By having music in the classroom, a positive emotional environment conducive to learning can be created. Lay the foundations of musical intelligence in your classroom by using music throughout the school day.

Interpersonal Intelligence

Interpersonal intelligence consists of:

- the ability to focus outward to other individuals
- the ability to sense other people's moods, temperaments, motivations, and intentions
- the ability to communicate, cooperate, and collaborate with others

In the early form of this intelligence, a young child possesses the ability to discriminate among the individuals around him or her and to detect their various moods. In the more advanced form of this intelligence, one can read the intentions and desires of other individuals and act upon that knowledge. This intelligence includes the ability to form and maintain relationships and to assume various roles within groups. The competence is prominent in political and religious leaders, salespeople, teachers, counselors, social workers, and therapists.

Interpersonally skilled people have the capacity to influence their peers and often excel at group work, team efforts, and collaborative projects. They enjoy social interaction and are sensitive to the feelings and moods of others. They tend to take leadership roles in activities with friends and often belong to clubs and other organizations.

Interpersonal intelligence can be developed and strengthened through maintaining a warm, accepting, supporting classroom environment. Provide opportunities for students to collaboratively work in groups. Have students peer teach and contribute to group discussions. Involve the students in situations where they have to be active listeners, be aware of other's feelings, motives, and opinions, and show empathy.

The positive development of interpersonal intelligence is an important step toward leading a successful and fulfilling life. Interpersonal intelligence is called upon in our daily lives as we interact with others in our communities, environments, nations, and world.

Intrapersonal Intelligence

Intrapersonal intelligence consists of:

- the ability to look inward to examine one's own thoughts and feelings
- the ability to control one's thoughts and emotions and consciously work with them
- the ability to express one's inner life
- the drive toward self-actualization

This intelligence focuses on the ability to develop a complete model of oneself, including one's desires, goals, anxieties, strengths, and limitations, and also to draw upon that model as a means of understanding and guiding one's behavior. In its basic form, it is the ability to distinguish a feeling of pleasure from one of pain, and to make a determination to either continue or withdraw from a situation based on this feeling. In the more advanced form of this intelligence, one has the ability to detect and to symbolize complex and highly differentiated sets of feelings. Some individuals with strong intrapersonal intelligence are philosophers, spiritual counselors, psychiatrists, and wise elders.

Intrapersonally skilled people are aware of their range of emotions and have a realistic sense of their strengths and weaknesses. They prefer to work independently and often have their own style of living and learning. They are able to accurately express their feelings and have a good sense of self-direction. They possess high self-confidence.

Intrapersonal intelligence can be developed through maintaining a warm, caring, nurturing environment that promotes self-esteem. Offer activities that require independent learning and imagination. During the school day, provide students with quiet time and private places to work and reflect. Provide long-term, meaningful learning projects that allow students to explore their interests and abilities. Encourage students to maintain portfolios and examine and make sense of their work. Involve students in activities that require them to explore their values, beliefs, and feelings.

Intrapersonal intelligence requires a lifetime of living and learning to inwardly know, be, and accept oneself. The classroom is a place where teachers can help students begin this journey of self-knowledge. Developing intrapersonal intelligence has far-reaching effects, since self-knowledge underlies success and fulfillment in life.

Naturalist Intelligence

Naturalist intelligence consists of:

- the ability to understand, appreciate, and enjoy the natural world
- the ability to observe, understand, and organize patterns in the natural environment
- the ability to nurture plants and animals

This intelligence focuses on the ability to recognize and classify the many different organic and inorganic species. Paleontologists, forest rangers, horticulturists, zoologists, and meteorologists exhibit naturalist intelligence.

People who exhibit strength in the naturalist intelligence are very much at home in nature. They enjoy being outdoors, camping, and hiking, as well as studying and learning about animals and plants. They can easily classify and identify various species.

Naturalist intelligence can be developed and strengthened through activities that involve hands-on labs, creating classroom habitats, caring for plants and animals, and classifying and discriminating species. Encourage your students to collect and classify seashells, insects, rocks, or other natural phenomena. Visit a museum of natural history, a university life sciences department, or nature center.

Naturalist intelligence enhances our lives. The more we know about the natural world, and the more we are able to recognize patterns in our environment, the better perspective we have on our role in natural cycles and our place in the universe.

REFERENCES

Armstrong, Thomas. *Multiple Intelligences in the Classroom*. Alexandria, VA: Assoc. for Supervision and Curriculum Development, 1994. A good overview of the Multiple Intelligences Theory and how to explore, introduce, and develop lessons on this theory.

Campbell, Linda, Bruce Campbell, and Dee Dickerson. *Teaching and Learning Through Multiple Intelligences*. Needham Heights, MA: Allyn and Bacon, 1996. An overview and resource of teaching strategies in musical, spatial, bodily-kinesthetic, interpersonal, and intrapersonal intelligences.

Gardner, Howard. *Frames of Mind: The Theory of Multiple Intelligences*. New York: Basic Books, 1993. A detailed analysis and explanation of the Multiple Intelligences Theory.

——. *Multiple Intelligences: The Theory in Practice*. New York: Basic Books, 1993. This book provides a coherent picture of what Gardner and his colleagues have learned about the educational applications of the Multiple Intelligences Theory over the last decade. It provides an overview of the theory and examines its implications for assessment and teaching from preschool to college admissions.

Haggerty, Brian A. *Nurturing Intelligences: A Guide to Multiple Intelligences Theory and Teaching*. Menlo Park, CA: Innovative Learning, Addison-Wesley, 1995. Principles, practical suggestions, and examples for applying the Multiple Intelligences Theory in the classroom. Exercises, problems, and puzzles introduce each of the seven intelligences.

Lazear, David. *Seven Pathways of Learning: Teaching Students and Parents About Multiple Intelligences*. Tucson: Zephyr Press, 1994. Assists in strengthening the child's personal intelligence and in integrating multiple intelligences into everyday life. Includes reproducibles and activities to involve parents.

——. *Seven Ways of Knowing: Teaching for Multiple Intelligences*. Arlington Heights, IL: IRI/SkyLight Training, 1992. A survey of the theory of multiple intelligences with many general activities for awakening and developing the intelligences.

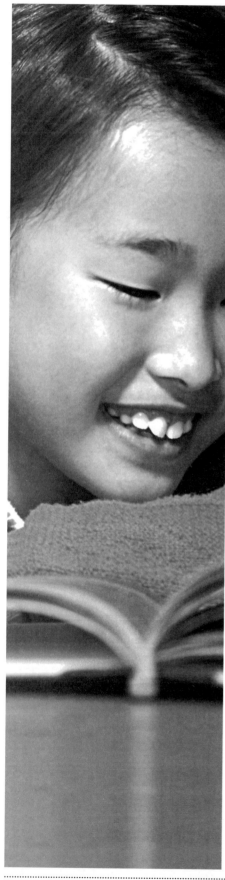

Verbal-Linguistic Intelligence

Color Words

Read to your class poems from the book *Hailstones and Halibut Bones: Adventures in Color,* by Mary O'Neill (Doubleday, 1989), as an introduction to this vocabulary activity. Then ask students to choose a color and write a paragraph using that color name frequently in description. Students will then think of nouns and adjectives that more precisely describe various shades of that color. (A thesaurus is helpful for this.) Finally, students should rewrite their paragraphs, substituting the more specific color words to refine their work.

Examples:

- The green bottle floated in the green sea near the green shore.

- The emerald-green bottle floated in the blue-green sea near the sage-colored shore.

- Her blue eyes reflected the blue pond.

- Her indigo eyes reflected the cerulean pond.

Language Roots

English has roots in Germanic, Latin, Greek, Anglo-Saxon, and many other languages. The Romance languages, based on Latin (or Roman), have many similarities, and by spelling and pronunciation, we can see where Latin and Romance languages have influenced English. The table below illustrates this.

English	amiable	love	to depart	eagle
Spanish	amable	amor	partir	aguila
French	aimable	amour	partir	aigle
Latin	amicare	amor	dispartire	aquila

English	verity	necessary	time	rose
Spanish	verdad	necesario	tiempo	rosa
French	verité	nécessaire	temps	rose
Latin	veritas	necessarius	tempus	rosa

Have students research words in foreign-language–English dictionaries to compare words from different languages. They can also research the English words in a dictionary to see where the words originated, and to identify similarities between languages.

Reading Aloud

Read aloud to your class each day for about twenty minutes. Choose classic children's stories or contemporary classics that will hook your students into the joys of great writing. Read books that some students might have difficulty reading on their own, but that they will enjoy. Pick some of your childhood favorites or consult with your school or local librarian. Some suggestions include: *A Wrinkle in Time*, by Madeline L'Engle (Farrar, Straus, Giroux, 1962), *Chitty-Chitty-Bang-Bang*, by Ian Fleming (Knopf, 1989), *The Indian in the Cupboard* series, by Lynne Reid Banks (Doubleday, 1985), and *The Forgotten Door*, by Alexander Key (Scholastic, 1986).

Many people can listen more effectively if they are allowed to doodle or draw at the same time they are listening. You may find some of your students are such listeners.

Logical-Mathematical Intelligence

Survey of Favorite Characters

In this activity students devise and conduct surveys and create bar graphs to present their data. Students should ask at least ten people who their favorite characters are in the following categories: fiction, nonfiction, cartoons, television shows, and movies. Students will have a more varied experience if at least one survey question is open-ended, and one close-ended.

Open-ended example: *Who is your favorite cartoon character?*

Close-ended example: *Which is your favorite movie character? Batman, R2D2 of* Star Wars, *Matilda, or Judy Jetson?*

There may be a greater range of answers for an open-ended question, which students will have to organize.

After they have concluded their survey, students should organize their information into bar graphs to present to the class—one bar graph per category. Discuss and analyze the experience of taking the survey, the kinds of questions that worked best, student opinions about why some questions worked better than others, how the students organized the data, and what they would do differently the next time.

Silly Ideas

To exercise students' logical thinking skills, brainstorm silly ideas and debate them. Some examples are:

- We should each remove one shoe each time we come into our classroom.

- Every bicycle in the world should be painted red.
- Students should wear umbrella hats on their heads at all times during the school day.

Students can develop arguments to support one or more of these silly ideas, and present their arguments to the whole class. Or students can break up into pairs or groups and debate.

Rhyme Patterns

Discuss the rhyme schemes of some favorite poems, using standard notation such as the following:

The Star

Twinkle, twinkle little star, (a)

How I wonder what you are! (a)

Up above the world so high, (b)

Like a diamond in the sky. (b)

As your bright and tiny spark, (c)

Lights the traveler in the dark— (c)

Though I know not what you are, (a)

Twinkle, twinkle little star. (a)

Have students pick other poems and analyze the rhyme schemes.

Bodily-Kinesthetic Intelligence

Clay Discovery

In this activity children will listen to and interpret instructions while working with clay. Give each student a ball of modeling clay. Explain that as they follow each step, they are not to break any piece of clay away from the mass.

Read aloud the following instructions and give students time to perform each:

- Change the shape of the clay by squeezing it.
- Pinch some of the clay so a couple of bulges stick out.
- Make a depression into the clay with a thumb.
- Pull out a piece of clay, stretching it into a long neck.
- Use a knuckle to poke more depressions into the clay.

· Change the shape in any way to suit yourself.

Students title their sculptures and present them. Compare and contrast the differences and similarities created by one set of instructions. Discuss the variety of sculptures students created based on their experience and aesthetic sense, and how the instructions were interpreted.

Texture Vocabulary

Brainstorm a list of texture words. Some words students might suggest are: *rough, scaly, dry, cracked, smooth, spiny, prickly, silky, soft,* and *bumpy.* A thesaurus can be used to find synonyms.

Divide the class into groups. Ask each group to produce a texture book that includes a collection of texture rubbings. Each texture rubbing is framed by words that describe that texture. Textures could be collected from the classroom, all over the school, or from home. Knit sweaters, soles of shoes, cardboard, wood, and many other substances can be used for rubbing. When the texture books are organized and compiled, groups can present their books and the new vocabulary words to the rest of the class.

Note: To make a rubbing, cover the textured surface with a piece of paper and color over it with the side of a crayon.

Punctuation Workout

Assign a physical action to punctuation marks and have the students practice them before doing the activity. The following are possible movements that can be assigned to each punctuation mark. They can be written on the board to help students remember.

· Period—clap hands over head.

· Exclamation mark—jump in place.

· Question mark—run in a small circle.

· Comma—spin around once.

After practicing the movements, read a paragraph, saying each punctuation mark as you come to it. Have students make the appropriate movement with each mark. Once students have mastered this, read a sentence to them but leave the punctuation marks out. Ask the students to signify the correct mark by making the appropriate movements.

Main Idea Pyramids

Using a story in your reading program, choose a simple paragraph and have students identify the main idea. On the chalkboard write down the main idea, using standard outline form. Have students identify two details in the paragraph that support the main idea, and add these to the outline.

Next choose one student to represent the main idea, and two to represent the supporting details. The two students representing details get on their hands and knees on the floor, and the student representing the main idea gets on top of them to make a pyramid. Discuss what would happen to the main idea if one of the details weren't strong enough, or were missing.

Continue identifying main ideas and details in the story with the class. You can also use this technique to analyze students' writing samples to help them see where they may need to strengthen their work.

Makeup Characters

In this activity students will make themselves up as characters—either taken from fiction or their own imaginations. Students can use theatrical makeup or nontoxic paint to create character makeup. After they have designed and made-up their faces in their new character, they write for five minutes about the character they have become. Then have the characters introduce themselves to the class, telling a little about themselves. Have two characters meet each other and converse about a topic for a couple of minutes. Some topic suggestions are: what home looks like, favorite pastimes of the characters, what they like to read, etc. Students will learn a lot about their character from this interaction.

Afterward students write again about their characters to develop more details based on what they learned during their conversation. Have them develop an adventure story in written or comic book form.

Body Spelling

For this activity groups of students will lie down to form letters with their bodies. For example, an M is formed with four students, two to form the sides of the M and two to make the inside V shape. Use this to study difficult spelling words. As students make the letters, take a picture of each letter. Combine them to create the spelling words and post them in the classroom.

Visual-Spatial Intelligence

Package Design

Display a variety of product packages for the class, such as cereal boxes, book covers, toy boxes, and pen packaging. Discuss how the words on the package look and how they create interest in the product. Then students can choose or invent a product to package. Discuss how and where they will sell it, as, for example, packages and products destined for a bookstore generally are not similar to those sold in a large grocery store.

Next students will design packages in which to market their products. Consideration should be given to what the components of the package will be, such as plastic bubbles, a cardboard box with cardboard cover, or a hard tin. Have students write the words, called copy, and design the illustrations for the package. Copy should explain what the product is and why the consumer would want to own it. Illustrations should show the product, and how it is used.

Then the class can construct the package and add the copy and the illustrations. When the projects are completed have students share them with the class.

Map the Classics

Choose a familiar story that has more than one location, such as "The Three Little Pigs." Draw or sketch the first location on the chalkboard. As students take turns reading the story, they add sketches of new scenes to the map on the board. When the story is finished, the students make their own maps, either copying and embellishing the one done as a class, or drawing a map of their own favorite story. Use the **Map the Classics** worksheet found on page 20.

Make Bookmarks

Use the **Make Bookmarks** worksheet found on page 21 to promote student reading and provide a quick summary of important language arts information. After students create, color, and cut out their bookmarks, they can be laminated for greater durability.

Emergency Map

Have students make a map of their home with all exits clearly marked. Ask them to write an emergency plan detailing the steps their family members would take in the event of a natural disaster or a fire in their home. Include a list of emergency supplies and where they are located, a list of important

page 20

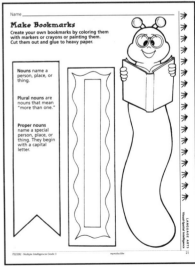

page 21

items to save if time allows, and information such as the emergency number to call—911—and relatives' phone numbers.

Musical Intelligence

Radio Program Magic

Play a tape of a radio drama such as "The Lone Ranger," "Lights Out," or "War of the Worlds," or a fully dramatized book on tape. These tapes are usually available at a local library. Talk about sound effects and how they improve the performance.

- A rain effect is created by a large cone of waxed paper held at an angle. Salt is sprinkled into the top of the cone so that it runs down the inside.
- A thunder effect is created by shaking a thin, flexible, metal baking sheet.
- An ocean effect is created by putting 1/4 cup of dried peas into a plastic bowl and tilting the bowl slowly from side to side so that the peas slide back and forth.
- Fire sounds are created by crumpling a cellophane bag.
- A jet plane sound can be re-created by running a blow dryer at low speed.
- Horse hoof sounds can be created by tapping two coconut halves together.

Students can reproduce these sound effects and create their own to enhance a radio play that they write and perform. They can keep track of the sound effects created and the materials they used on the **Radio Program Magic** worksheet found on page 22.

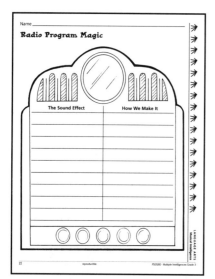

page 22

Dancing Poetry

To engage students' musical and verbal abilities, read a poem to them and make up movements to emphasize the rhyme and rhythm of it.

My name is Don Paul,

I'm not very tall.

My home is a hut,

My dog is a mutt.

If you love to eat peas,

Come visit me, please.

While listening to the poem above, the students can revolve slowly in a circle. At the end of each line, the students hop while you say the last word. Students can also tap their feet to the beat and clap on the last word of each line. Extensions of this activity include using more than one student to create a choreographed version of a poem, using different readers, choral reading effects, and classroom instruments to keep the beat. Poems by Jack Prelutsky, Jane Yolen, and A.A. Milne are useful for this activity.

Rhythmic Reminders

Whenever students have a particularly difficult time remembering vocabulary words, mathematical equations, or other facts, help them develop a short rhythmic reminder, such as:

- 3 times 3 is 9; 9 makes me feel fine.
- 8 by 8 fell on the floor; when they got up they were 64!
- In 1492, Columbus sailed the ocean blue!

Interpersonal Intelligence

Class Portraits

Create a silhouette of each student either freehand or using an overhead projector to cast a shadow of the student, which can be traced on a piece of paper taped on the wall. Label each drawing with the student's name. Pass the silhouettes out to the class, assigning one randomly to each child.

Ask students to search through magazines, newspapers, and junk mail to look for complimentary nouns, gerunds, and adjectives to describe their classmates. After students have collected approximately five words, have them arrange the words in a pleasing design and glue them to the paper around the silhouette. Each portrait can be signed by the student. Display the class portraits in a public area.

Homophone Teams

Have groups of students brainstorm as many homophones as they can. Some pairs of words to get them started are:

air, heir	ate, eight	you, ewe
I, eye	ball, bawl	carrot, carat
gnu, new	leak, leek	sealing, ceiling

Have student teams design and illustrate posters to help them identify the words. Special word posters can be made for other confusing spelling words as well.

Special Interest Communications

Encourage students to form clubs to pursue a special interest while developing their language skills. Examples are a Reading Club, an Internet Club, or a Soccer Club. The students can develop organization rules, define their purpose, goals, and objectives, and write, edit, and publish a newsletter and calendar for their club. These can be distributed to members and other interested parties, and posted on a community board.

Intrapersonal Intelligence

EQ

Brainstorm a list of emotions with the class. Some suggestions are: happiness, sadness, pride, frustration, envy, bitterness, joy, and anger. Discuss that sometimes we can feel two different emotions about the same event; for example, excitement about going on a trip, but fear about going to an unfamiliar place. Talk about how conflicting emotions are human, and explore how they feel.

Develop strategies that students could use to deal with conflicting emotions. Some suggestions might be: writing in a journal about the feelings, creating a comic strip about the worst and best things that could happen, discussing the feelings with a trusted friend or adult, or listening to quiet music with eyes closed.

Pet Eulogies

Read aloud *The Tenth Good Thing About Barney*, by Judith Viorst (Atheneum, 1971). Find out how many students have had a pet die and let some tell their stories. Explain that a eulogy is a speech or writing in praise of a dead person. Have students write a eulogy for their pets. Discuss what kinds of things could be written in the eulogy. Some suggestions that the students might make include:

· where their pet came from

· what their pet was like

· how their pet changed as it grew

· how their pet got its name

- their pet's favorite toy, food, or game

- who or what their pet didn't like

- special tricks their pet could do

- who took care of their pet

- experiences that their pet had with neighbors

- experiences that their pet had at a kennel, getting lost, or going to the vet

- funny things their pet did

After the students have written the eulogies, encourage them to share them with the class.

Naturalist Intelligence

Listen to Nature

This activity is a variation on a word web. It can help expand your students' vocabulary while at the same time increase their awareness of sounds in nature. This activity can be done on a large piece of paper. Choose a natural setting and write it in a large flower, as shown at right. Add a stem to the flower. Then add lines to the stem. On these lines write a natural object or phenomenon, such as *waves* or *sea gulls*, and write the sound it produces on the other side. Brainstorm with students and have them write the words *whoosh, screech, rumbles, giggle, plunk,* or other words. Keep the completed flower and others created by the class on display so they can be referred to during reading and writing time. Different topics can be applied to this activity, such as animal noises or colors, textures in the natural world, tastes of fruit and vegetables, etc.

Smell the Roses

Give your students an opportunity to "stop and smell the roses" and put the experience into words. As a homework assignment or during a field trip to a park or other natural setting, have students observe nature and record what they see, hear, touch, smell, and taste. These five sense words can be written on a piece of paper, leaving space for observations. The paper can be titled according to the setting. For example, a title could be *A Walk in the Bird Sanctuary*. Next to the word *touch* could be written: *soft, ticklish feathers, dry, crinkly leaves, damp, cold rock,* and so on.

Map the Classics

Draw a map of the locations of your favorite story.

MAP

of _____

N
W · E
S

reproducible

LANGUAGE ARTS
Visual-Spatial Intelligence

Make Bookmarks

Create your own bookmarks by coloring them with markers or crayons or painting them. Cut them out and glue to heavy paper.

Nouns name a person, place, or thing.

Plural nouns are nouns that mean "more than one."

Proper nouns name a special person, place, or thing. They begin with a capital letter.

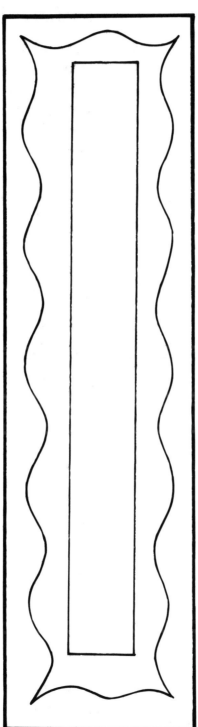

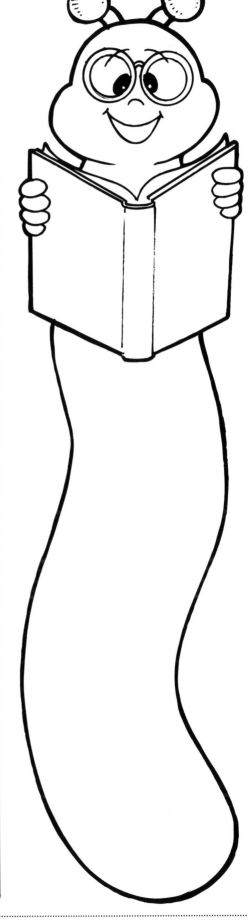

LANGUAGE ARTS
Visual-Spatial Intelligence

Radio Program Magic

The Sound Effect	How We Make It

reproducible

LANGUAGE ARTS
Musical Intelligence

Verbal-Linguistic Intelligence

Community Service

Invite one or more community service volunteers to visit the class. Your visitor could explain different volunteer opportunities, why people volunteer, how others benefit from the service, and the rewards of being a volunteer.

Ahead of time students can brainstorm a list of questions to ask the visitor. Assist the students in writing their questions clearly so they are prepared for the visitor. Some sample questions are:

- Why did you want to be a volunteer?
- What do you do on a typical day?
- What is your favorite part of the job?
- What's the most important thing you learned in school that helps you do your job?

Have students write an essay after the volunteer has spoken to the class.

Logical-Mathematical Intelligence

Occupations in Our Community

In this activity students conduct surveys to explore the kinds of occupations that exist in their community. First review different occupations and categories with the class, using the list below. Assist the students in thinking of other occupations that fit each category. Then pass out the **Occupations in Our Community** worksheet, found on page 30. Have students gather occupational data and fill in the worksheet on a field trip, or as homework assignments.

page 30

Compile the data and classify it into the categories of service, sales, production, operations, administration. Develop a simple pie chart to compare the totals of workers by category.

service—teacher

sales—cashier

production—graphic artist

operations—factory worker

administration—manager

Graph of Highest and Lowest Points on Earth

Use a map or a globe to show students the Himalayas mountain range in Asia, which has the highest peak in the world—Mount Everest, 29,028 feet above sea level. Make a horizontal line in the middle of the chalkboard that represents sea level, and draw a tall mountain shape. Label the mountain 29,028 ft.

Next point out the lowest point on earth, the Mariana Trench near the island of Guam in the Pacific Ocean. The deepest part of the Mariana Trench is 36,201 feet below sea level. Add the valley to your chalkboard drawing below sea level and label it 36,201 ft.

Then present information about the elevation of your community and label the chalkboard drawing accordingly.

Ask students to make a graph to show the highest and lowest points on earth and the elevation of your community. Hand out graph paper and have everyone draw a horizontal line in the middle of a page to represent sea level. Next students should decide how large to make the increments on the graph. Point out that if they decide to make each horizontal line on the graph paper equal to one foot, they will run out of room on their paper. Help students figure out how many feet each line will represent (2,000 or 3,000 feet are easy increments to use). Students should create their graph by writing the increments on each graph line. Then put a dot at the correct spot above sea level for Mount Everest, a second dot below sea level for the Mariana Trench, and a dot representing your community in the appropriate place.

Students can draw a mountain, trench, or elevated area on the graph similar to the illustration at left. Then the graph should be labeled.

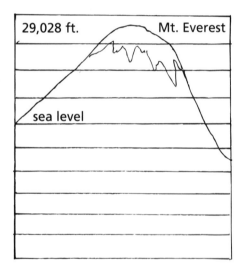

29,028 ft. Mt. Everest

sea level

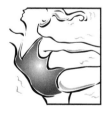

Bodily-Kinesthetic Intelligence

Messages in Braille

Introduce students to communication by means of the Braille language code, used by blind people who read by feeling the raised dots with their fingers. Braille was invented by Louis Braille in 1824 when he was 15 years old, and is based on a "cell" of six dots. Braille worked out an alphabet, punctuation marks, numerals, and a system of writing music from the 63 possible combinations of dots. It is used for all written languages and for mathematics, science, and computer notation.

Distribute the **Messages in Braille** worksheet found on page 31. Have students write their names in Braille on a separate piece of paper using white or colored glue to make the dots. If they add a little sand or other texture to the glue, it may be easier to feel the dots. Toothpicks can be used to apply the glue. Students can also encode a message in Braille for another student to decipher.

Signing

Sign language is the language of gestures and hand signals used by deaf and hard-of-hearing people to communicate. There are a number of different sign languages. There is also a manual "finger" alphabet used to finger spell words. They are used in combination with gestures for specific words or names.

The American manual alphabet can be found in the *World Book Encyclopedia* (World Book, 1995) article titled "Sign Language" (Vol. 17, page 453), or *The Macmillan Visual Desk Reference* (Macmillan, 1993). Show students how to spell their names using the manual alphabet. Then students can learn to form the manual letters and practice spelling short sign language conversations with each other.

Visual-Spatial Intelligence

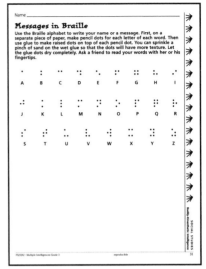

page 31

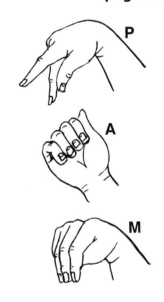

Terrain Model of the Local Region

Take a field trip to explore, observe, and study the local environment. Augment the field trip with maps, videos, slides, and photographs of the local region. Before embarking on this project, students should be able to identify the natural features of your region (such as hills, mountains, lakes, rivers, and coastline). Have students construct a topographical map of the region. Materials that can be used to make the model are ceramic clay, salt clay, modeling clay, plaster of Paris, papier-mâché, local rocks, mixed media, or found materials. The models can be built on a tray, inside a cardboard box or other container.

This topographical map can be used as the basis to consider local history. Where did people live and why? Where are the water sources? What are different ways land has been used through time? How has its physical geography affected the region? How are topographical features being used today?

Student Compasses

Invite students to play a directional game based on "Simon Says." First locate and label north in the classroom. Then have students stand. Explain that you will be giving geographical directions. If a direction is preceded by the words "Atlas says...," students are to turn and face that way. If the suggestion is not preceded by those words, students should ignore it. Begin with simple directions—east, west, etc. Then move on to intermediate directions—northwest, southeast, north-northeast, east-southeast, and so on.

Map Puzzles

Reproduce maps of geographical areas the class is studying, or use old maps. Invite students to create jigsaw puzzles from the maps. First maps should be glued to a stiff paper backing. When the glue is dry, maps can be cut into irregular pieces. Store each map puzzle in a separate plastic bag or manila envelope labeled with the city, country, or continent it features.

Musical Intelligence

Make Maracas

Maracas make a distinctive sound and are easy to pick out in Latin-American music. They are also simple to make and fun to play. Students need yogurt containers or liquid detergent bottles, masking tape, strong brown paper, and material to fill the maraca, such as handfuls of dried beans, peas, lentils, rice, or gravel. Make sure the containers or strainers are dry, fill them with a handful of rattling material, and seal well. Cover the container with brown paper using tape. The maraca can be decorated with papier-mâché or glued decorations.

Interpersonal Intelligence

What Is Intelligence?

Research the word *intelligence* in the dictionary and share it with the class. Then brainstorm student ideas about intelligence. Questions to consider are:

· How do you know if someone is intelligent?

· How do intelligent people behave?

· How do people become intelligent?

Talk in broad terms about the different strengths people have, such as drawing, sports, writing, reading, inventing things (mechanical or imaginary), doing math problems, getting along with people and helping people get along together, and musical ability.

List Howard Gardner's eight multiple intelligences on the board and give examples of each. For example, under *bodily-kinesthetic,* list *ballet dancer, marathon runner, rock climber.* Have groups of students make posters listing or portraying well-known people in each intelligence category. Also, have students write about how they use each intelligence in their own life.

Tools for Conflict Resolution

This activity offers a way to resolve conflicts among students. Explain to students that when conflicts occur, it is a good idea to try and see the issue through the other person's eyes. Considering the different perspectives of a conflict can open up one's mind, foster empathy, and help the conflicting parties find a middle point at which to meet. Using the **Masks** worksheet found on page 32, have students create self-portraits in mask form. Store the masks in a secure place in the classroom to use as tools when conflicts arise.

When students encounter conflict, they exchange masks. With the masks held in front of their faces, students take turns stating the problem as the other person sees it.

When all parties have spoken they put the masks aside. Then each person states how he or she is responsible for the problem. The class and the students in conflict brainstorm solutions and choose a solution that satisfies both.

A good resource about conflict resolution and peacemaking is *Learning the Skills of Peacemaking,* by Naomi Drew (Jalmar Press, 1987).

page 32

A Valuable Person

Share with the class a personal story about an important person in your life who has taught you something valuable. Then ask students to make a list of people important to them and what the people have taught them.

Using the **A Valuable Person** worksheet on page 33, have students interview one of the important people on their list. They can draw a picture or put a photocopy of a photo of the person in the frame on the worksheet.

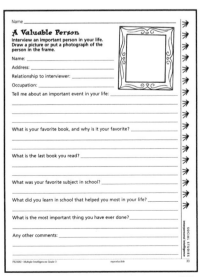

page 33

Intrapersonal Intelligence

Monuments for Ourselves

Read the book *Wonderful Tower of Watts* by Patricia Zelver (Morrow, 1994). The Watts Towers were built by Simon Rodia, who came from Italy and lived in a poor neighborhood in Los Angeles. All the objects on the towers are recycled from things thrown away. Initiate a discussion about what the towers say about Simon Rodia.

Have students design and execute a miniature monument to themselves. Some things that students might consider while designing the monuments are:

- the kind of person they are or want to be
- where they live now and have lived in the past
- what they like to do, such as sports or hobbies
- what they want to do in the future
- favorite books, toys, or characters

The miniature monuments can be created with a base such as a cardboard box that objects are attached to. Or objects can be simply piled into a form. Possible objects are: discarded clothing, hats, or shoes; postcards, letters, schoolwork, journal pages; toys; natural objects such as pine cones or seashells; souvenirs; sports equipment such as tennis balls, bats, uniforms, etc.

After students have created their monuments, invite other classes to view the projects. Then discuss what the students learned about themselves from creating their monuments.

Setting Personal Goals

At the beginning of a new unit of study, encourage students to set personal goals for their own learning. Discuss the kinds of goals they may want to consider: to learn something specific, to read three good books about a topic, to finish a project within the given time frame, to work cooperatively in a group, and so on. Have each student record his or her goal on a slip of paper. Then ask them to put the papers in a safe place. At the end of the unit, have students review their goals and reflect upon whether or not they were achieved. Encourage students to share their reflections in writing.

Naturalist
Intelligence

Biodiversity

Study biodiversity with your class by reading *Living Treasure: Saving Earth's Threatened Biodiversity,* by Laurence Pringle (Morrow, 1991). Other good resources are *Biodiversity,* by Dorothy Henshaw Patent (Clarion, 1996), and *Bats, Bugs, and Biodiversity: Adventures in the Amazonian Rain Forest,* by Susan Goodman (Atheneum, 1995).

Explain to your class that humans also exhibit the characteristics of biodiversity; some have freckles, some have red hair, some are green eyed, etc.

Create a biodiversity display in your classroom that can be developed throughout the year. Start by observing the human biodiversity in the classroom. Take photos of some children's hands, some children's eyes, other children's smiles. Make sure all children are represented. Mount these photos for all to appreciate each child's individuality.

Add to the biodiversity display by having children collect any of the following: seashells, pine cones, leaves, bugs, nuts, feathers, and other objects from nature. Point out to students that there is diversity within each species as well as among them.

Earth Day Challenge

Read to your class *Earth Day,* by Linda Lowery (Carolrhoda, 1991), a short book about the history of Earth Day. Tell your class how Earth Day is observed in your community. Challenge students as individuals to change one habit in their lives that will help preserve the planet. Then challenge the class as a group to make a change that will benefit the natural world.

Nature's Cuisine

Teach your students about the plants and animals of the countries they are studying in social studies. Make a list of which plants and animals provide food for the people of these countries. Introduce to your class meals that are prepared using these products. With the class create a menu for breakfast, lunch, and dinner using these products. Provide some of these foods for the class to enjoy on an "International Food Day."

Occupations in Our Community

Ask a worker in your community these questions.

Survey Questions

What is your job title? _____

_____

What do you do on your job? _____

_____

What special skills do you use? _____

_____

What education would I need to do your job? _____

_____

Other survey questions: _____

_____

_____

_____

_____

_____

_____

_____

How would you classify your job?

Service   Sales   Production

Operations   Administration

Name _____

Messages in Braille

Use the Braille alphabet to write your name or a message. First, on a separate piece of paper, make pencil dots for each letter of each word. Then use glue to make raised dots on top of each pencil dot. You can sprinkle a pinch of sand on the wet glue so that the dots will have more texture. Let the glue dots dry completely. Ask a friend to read your words with her or his fingertips.

A B C D E F G H I

J K L M N O P Q R

S T U V W X Y Z

SOCIAL STUDIES
Bodily-Kinesthetic Intelligence

Name _____

Masks

Decorate the mask to look like you. Glue the mask onto thick paper. Cut out the face and create holes for the eyes. Attach a craft stick along one side of the mask to use as a holder.

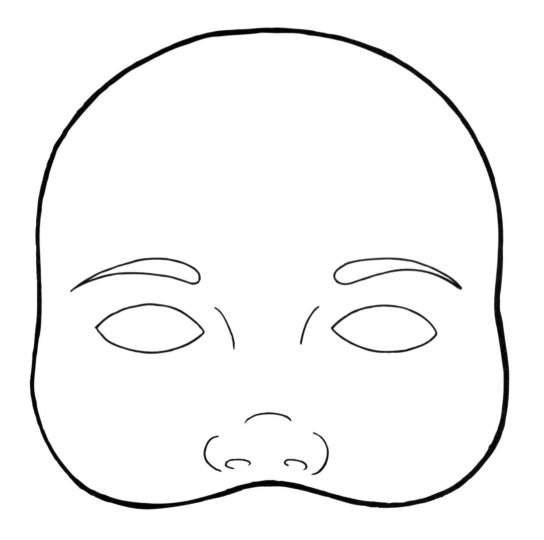

reproducible

SOCIAL STUDIES
Interpersonal Intelligence

Name _____

A Valuable Person

Interview an important person in your life. Draw a picture or put a photograph of the person in the frame.

Name: _____

Address: _____

Relationship to interviewer: _____

Occupation: _____

Tell me about an important event in your life: _____

_____

_____

What is your favorite book, and why is it your favorite? _____

_____

_____

What is the last book you read? _____

_____

What was your favorite subject in school? _____

_____

What did you learn in school that helped you most in your life? _____

_____

What is the most important thing you have ever done? _____

_____

Any other comments: _____

_____

SOCIAL STUDIES
Interpersonal Intelligence

Verbal-Linguistic Intelligence

Create a Word Problem Bank

Write a mathematical formula on the chalkboard such as $x + y = z$. Then write a word problem based on the formula.

Example: Lorraine had 35 fossils in her rock collection. When she went on vacation with her family to Wyoming, she acquired 17 more specimens. After she returned home, how many rocks did she have in all?

Have students write original word problems based on the formula. Provide an index card for each student. Students will then write the problem on one side and the answer on the back. File the problems in a Word Problem Bank card file. Use the student-written problems for practice and for tests.

Word Logic

Use verbal equations to replace mathematical ones. Write an example on the chalkboard, such as $c = a + b$ or $x - y = z$. If your students are unfamiliar with the use of variable notation (a, b, c, x, y, z), use number sentences such as $3 + 5 = 8$ and $6 - 1 = 5$. Point out that verbal phrases can show similar logic, such as the following:

- ice cream + cone = ice cream cone
- rain + sunshine = rainbow
- water = ice + freezing temperature

Encourage students to create their own logic phrases. The equations can be written in words, as in the above example, or in pictures.

Here's How I Did It

Students can clarify their thinking and improve their ability to verbalize problem-solving strategies by explaining how they solved a difficult math problem. Pair up students and have them discuss their methods with each other. Writing their explanation is another way to practice math vocabulary.

Describe a Solid

Gather several manipulatives of the three-dimensional solids (cubes, triangular prisms, rectangular prisms, cylinders, and pyramids). Put one example of each kind of solid in view of the students and the rest into a grocery bag.

One student reaches inside the bag, chooses an object and, while continuing to hide it, describes the solid to the other students. Encourage students to use the correct mathematical language to tell about their solid, such as faces, corners, and edges.

Number Scavenger Hunt

This activity will show students how numbers are integrated into daily life. Decide on several categories of numbers to be sought. Some suggestions are: the price of food, an address, a number in a shoe or clothing size, a telephone number, a date, a number in a recipe, etc.

Divide the class into groups. Each group will need newspapers and magazines, glue, crayons, and paper on which to paste their finds. The group searches in the printed matter to find examples of each category of number that has been chosen at the outset. The examples are cut out and pasted on the group's paper. When all papers have been completed, ask students to write a paragraph of how numbers are used in their lives.

Bodily-Kinesthetic Intelligence

Hopscotch Review

Lay out a hopscotch board using masking tape on the classroom floor or chalk on a paved area outside. Play the game by having students throw a marker or stone onto any space. They then follow the usual rules of hopscotch, hopping over that space on the way to the end and turning to make a return trip. Before picking up the marker or stone on the return trip, students must answer a review question based on the number in the square. For example, to review a family of multiplication facts, fill the squares with products and have the player supply a pair of factors that equal the number. To review fractions, write different fractions in each square. Then have players supply an equivalent fraction, a smaller fraction, a larger fraction, and so on.

Human Clocks

Tell the students that they are going to pretend that they are a clock, with their arms being the arms on the clock. Draw a large clock on the blackboard with the number in place but no arms. Have students stand and face the clock. Explain that at 12 o'clock their arms are straight above their heads with their hands together. Have the students show 12 o'clock. Model for students how to make their bodies show one o'clock—the left arm is straight above the head and the right arm slightly to the right. Have them move their arms to show one o'clock. Continue with the other hours. Call out a time and have the students place their arms in the correct position. To challenge students, have them show the time one hour later or two hours earlier than the time you say.

To extend this activity, go outside and let students work together to be a giant human clock that tells time to five minute intervals. Begin by writing large numbers from 1 to 12 on separate sheets of paper. Pass out a number sign to 12 students and have them arrange themselves in a large circle (sitting) to be the clock. Choose two more students—the taller one to be the minute hand and the shorter one to be the hour hand. Explain to these two students that you will call out a time and they are to lay down, feet to feet, inside the clock to show the time. Continue the activity rotating children so everyone has the opportunity to be a number or a hand on the clock.

Proof in the Rice

Ask students how many 100s there are in 10,000. Have the class make predictions. Then explain that they are going to count to 10,000 by hundreds.

Divide the class into ten teams and provide each team with ten small plastic bags, one medium-sized plastic bag, tape, and rice. Each team makes ten bags with 100 pieces of rice in each bag. Put the small bags into the medium bag to make 1,000.

When teams are finished, go around the room and collect the medium-sized bags. Have students help you count out loud by thousands as you collect all ten medium-sized bags to make 10,000 pieces of rice.

Relay 1,000

This running activity familiarizes students with large numbers. Form student groups of 5 to run a relay race. Each group will run in place for 1,000 steps. Pose the following problem:

> Each person on your relay team has to take the same number of steps. How many steps does each member have to take? (200 steps)

When groups have determined their answer have them explain to the class how they figured it out.

Before the race, provide each team with a small object to use as a baton. Determine when the baton will be passed, such as each 100 steps, or after each person has completed 200 steps. After holding the relay race, discuss the event and the students' experience of 1,000. To extend the activity, repeat with teams of six (or another number that does not divide evenly into 1,000).

Place Value Playtime

Using place value blocks and two dice, ask students to race to see who can collect 1,000 first. This game can be played by two or more players. Create a bank of place value blocks in the center of the group of players. Each player takes a turn throwing the dice, adding the two numbers, and taking that number of place value blocks. Each time a player has ten 1-cubes, they are exchanged for a 10-bar. When a player has ten 10-bars, they are exchanged for a 100-square. The game continues until one person has reached 1,000.

What's Cooking?

Easy recipes can supply students with opportunities to measure and follow directions. Have students read a recipe for a favorite dish, make it, cook it, and eat it in the classroom. Some that can be made in an electric skillet with a thermostat and a lid are pancakes, one-pan corn bread, and pineapple upside-down cake. Consult your local library or bookstore for current children's cookbooks.

Visual-Spatial Intelligence

Tangrams

Working with tangrams is a fun activity that involves both logical-mathematical and spatial intelligence. On heavy tagboard, reproduce the **Tangram Puzzle** worksheet on page 44. Divide the class into small groups. Give each group a tangram puzzle, a pair of scissors, crayons, and a large sheet of butcher paper. Help the students name the various shapes in the tangram and examine how the pieces fit to make a square. Have one student cut out the pieces on the tagboard.

Here are tangram activities you can challenge groups to do. Have the groups show their answers on the butcher paper by tracing around the tagboard tangram pieces and labeling each with its matching number. They can reconstruct the shape with the paper pieces and glue them to a sheet of paper. End the activity by having groups display their papers and compare their results. Answers are on page 76.

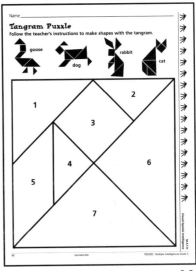

page 44

A. Make a square using two tangram pieces.

B. Make a triangle using two tangram pieces.

C. Make a square using three tangram pieces.

D. Make a rectangle using three tangram pieces.

E. Make a triangle using three tangram pieces.

F. Make a square using the five smaller tangram pieces.

G. Make a square using all the tangram pieces.

H. Use as many pieces as possible to create an animal or an object, such as the ones pictured on the worksheet. Use crayons to trace, color, and add features to your creation.

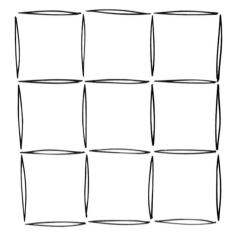

Squares of Squares

Arrange children in pairs and give each pair 24 toothpicks. Ask them to arrange the toothpicks as shown at left. Then have partners count to determine the number of squares made by the toothpicks. If a pair counts nine squares, tell them to count again. Help them understand that any four small squares can be combined to make a large square. And the entire design makes an even larger square. (The answer is 14 different squares. The small squares in the middle columns are counted as part of more than one square. And the entire shape makes up a square.)

Provide each pair with 12 additional toothpicks and ask them to create an even larger square of squares. (The new square will have to be four toothpicks long on each side.) Then repeat the counting exercise.

Nets

This activity explores nets. A net of a solid is the plane shape. When the plane shape is cut out and folded, it can be made into a solid shape.

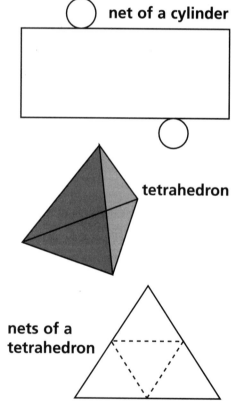

net of a cylinder

tetrahedron

nets of a tetrahedron

From a collection of cardboard boxes have each student select a box to cut open so that it can be flattened into one piece. Encourage students to cut open their boxes in different ways. Have them lay out their flattened figure on a desk or tabletop. Tell them these are called nets. Select one of the nets and ask the class to predict what kind of box could be made from it. Have one student remake the box from the net and show it to the class.

Show the class a regular tetrahedron. Ask them to visualize what the net would look like and have them draw it freehand. There are two possibilities, as shown at left.

Pass out eleven pieces of grid paper to each student. (The larger squares work best for this activity.) Ask the class to look at a cube and draw some of the possible nets of it. Have students cut out and fold their nets to verify whether a cube can be completed from it. Challenge the students to find as many of the eleven possible nets as they can and verify by folding. Display the student solutions on the bulletin board.

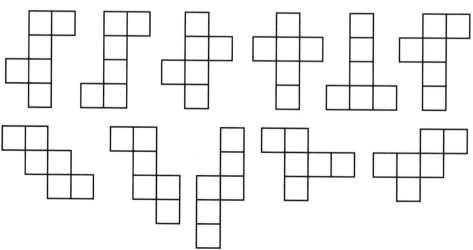

nets of cubes

The Magic Grid

A grid placed over a drawing breaks the design into small pieces that can be enlarged or shrunk easily. Draw and label a sample grid and dragon on the chalkboard or use an overhead projector and a transparency made from the **Draw a Bigger Dragon** worksheet found on page 45.

Pass out the worksheet to the class, and then show students how to use the horizontal and vertical coordinates to locate one square on the small grid, and then the corresponding square on the larger grid. Then copy the line located in that square on the smaller grid into the corresponding square on the larger grid.

Once students have completed the dragon drawing, they can find other drawings to make, using the grid worksheet.

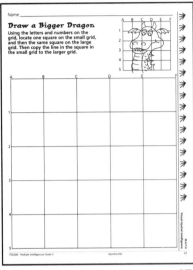

page 45

Three-D Magic

In this worksheet activity students use color to create drawings that seem to rise off the page. Each student needs a piece of white paper, a blue highlighter marker and a pink highlighter marker, and a 2-by-2-inch square each of blue and red translucent plastic. Plastic report covers can be used for the translucent plastic sheets.

Have students trace the drawing on the **Three-D Magic** worksheet found on page 46. They should use pink highlighter to trace and color the stars, and blue highlighter to trace the lines and outline the stars. When finished drawing, they close their left eye and look at the drawing through the red plastic with their right eye. Then they close their right eye and look at the drawing through the blue plastic piece. Finally, they look through both eyes with the red plastic over the right eye, and the blue plastic over the left eye.

When looked at through both colors, the image changes. The red plastic will filter out most of the pink, and the right eye will see dark stars. The blue plastic will filter out most of the blue, and the left eye will see dark lines. When both colors are used at the same time, the brain is tricked by the eyes into seeing an optical illusion. Each eye sends a different image, and the brain puts them both together, creating the 3-D effect.

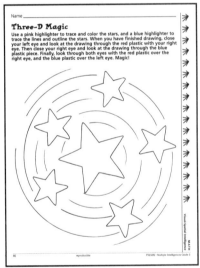

page 46

Musical Intelligence

Rhythmic Skip Counting

Demonstrate a simple rhythm pattern such as:

clap-clap-snap, clap-clap-snap, clap-clap-snap

(clap = clap your hands together, snap = snap your fingers)

Repeat the rhythm several times with your students until they are comfortable with it. Pair students to practice skip counting by twos to this rhythm as they perform the hand movements. The first student says 2, 4 while clapping twice, and the partner says 6 while snapping once. They continue skip counting in rhythm to a preset number. Extend the activity with different skip counting patterns and different rhythms.

Singing Patterns

Sing with a simple word pattern such as *red, blue, red, blue, red, blue*. Sing the word *red* with one note, and the word *blue* with another. Extend the pattern to *red, yellow, blue,* and later, *red, yellow, green, blue*. For both these patterns each color has its own note. Have students join you in the singing.

After students are comfortable recognizing these relatively simple audio patterns, change to a numeric format such as 2, 4, **1**, 6, 8, **2**, 10, 12, **3**, 14, 16, **4**, etc. This pattern has two parts: the even number series intermingled with the counting number series (the latter are in bold type). Sing the pattern representing the even numbers with one note per number, and the counting numbers with a different note.

Extend the activity by using instruments to play the different components of the patterns.

Interpersonal Intelligence

Student Teacher

Schedule each student to teach a math lesson. The day before the lesson, review the lesson with the student. It is also useful to review classroom management techniques, including speaking loudly and slowly enough, the importance of involving all students in the lesson, and how to respond to correct and incorrect answers. This activity can be used successfully in other subject areas as well.

Shopping Lesson

Collect a variety of toys and books and assign a price to each item. Set them up in a classroom store. Divide the class into groups of approximately four students. One student shopper from each group is given a spending limit. Allow the shoppers two minutes to purchase as many items as they can without exceeding their limit. Group members can help estimate totals. When the time is up, students return to their groups and total the purchases. Continue the activity until all students have had a chance to shop.

Strategic Thinking with Checkers

Pair students to play checkers against each other. After each game, pairs analyze and discuss the strategy the winner used to win. After two games they switch partners and continue the play and analysis. At the end of the allotted time, reunite the class and have a group discussion about the strategies they discovered.

Intrapersonal Intelligence

Reflecting on Making Math Mistakes

Encourage students to write in their journals, or write a private paragraph, about how they feel when they get a math answer wrong.

As a group, reflect on strategies that can help prevent mistakes. Some suggestions may include: practicing the facts, reading problems carefully to find the question that must be answered, checking answers, and so on. Have students make posters to hang in the room as reminders of the strategies they have explored.

Survival Budgets

Provide photocopies of catalog pages to each student that offer a variety of consumer goods. Camping gear, clothing, sports equipment, and book catalogs would be appropriate for the activity. With a budget of $250, students prepare a provisions list (food and water not included on the list) for a two-month stay on an island where there is no electricity. Discuss their reasons for making their choices. Why did they choose what they chose? How would their choices change if their budgets were $500 or if their stay were extended to six months? Would they make different choices if their families were with them? What about the choices they would make if a friend were with them? Have students answer these questions in an essay.

Personal Math Goals

Setting personal math goals can accelerate students' progress by challenging students and giving them an opportunity to feel pride in meeting their goals. Encourage students to set personal goals for learning multiplication and division facts. For example, if the class has regular timed tests on math facts, the students' goals can center on increasing the number of facts answered correctly. A student might set a goal to increase the amount of flash cards that can be solved correctly in a set amount of time.

Naturalist Intelligence

Nature's Geometry Scavenger Hunt

Arrange students into pairs or small groups and send them on a Nature's Geometry Scavenger Hunt. Students should search for some of the shapes, angles, and lines listed below in natural items such as the fork of tree branches, flowers, rocks, leaves, etc. Draw a picture of each item listed, and have the students draw them on their own list next to the words. Set the boundaries of the search area according to your circumstances, for example, the outside play area, a cross-country track, or a field trip site (or have them do the activity as homework at a natural site of their choosing). Vary your list according to terms taught.

Explain that groups must stay together as they search. They should check off each item found and note where the item was spotted. Set a time limit for the search. When the time is up, gather the groups together and see how many items were found by each group. Spot-check accuracy by asking each group to point to several of its finds. If some of the items on the list can't be found, discuss where one might find them in nature, such as seashells, spider webs, snowflakes, tornadoes, planets, etc.

Search for...

circle	right angle	cylinder
acute angle	horizontal line	rectangle
obtuse angle	vertical line	hexagon
semicircle	octagon	oval
cone	triangle	set of parallel lines
set of perpendicular lines		spiral

Weather Patterns

Have students keep track of the weather over a period of at least three weeks. Collect data about precipitation, extent and type of cloud cover, high and low temperatures, and wind speed and direction. Data can be a combination of observation, measurement, and use of published or broadcast weather reports. Keep track of the information on a class-sized weather chart.

At the end of the time period, have students study the data they collected to see if there are any patterns revealed. Did the air temperature seem to be affected by precipitation or the amount of cloud cover? Were specific cloud formations associated with specific weather phenomenon? Did wind direction appear to have anything to do with precipitation? Discuss the students' observations.

Fruit Kabob Patterns

Let each student make a fruit kabob to practice the concept of patterns. Each student will need freshly washed hands, a bamboo skewer, a paper plate, and a selection of bite-size fruit (such as peaches, apples, bananas, strawberries, watermelon, grapes, or pineapple). Model for students how to assemble a patterned fruit kabob by repeating fruit sequences. Then direct the students to create their own. Have the students share their fruit kabob patterns with their classmates. Finally, let the students eat their accomplishments!

Tangram Puzzle

Follow the teacher's instructions to make shapes with the tangram.

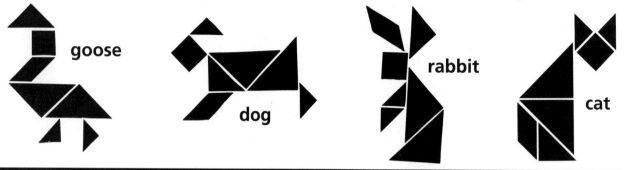

goose

dog

rabbit

cat

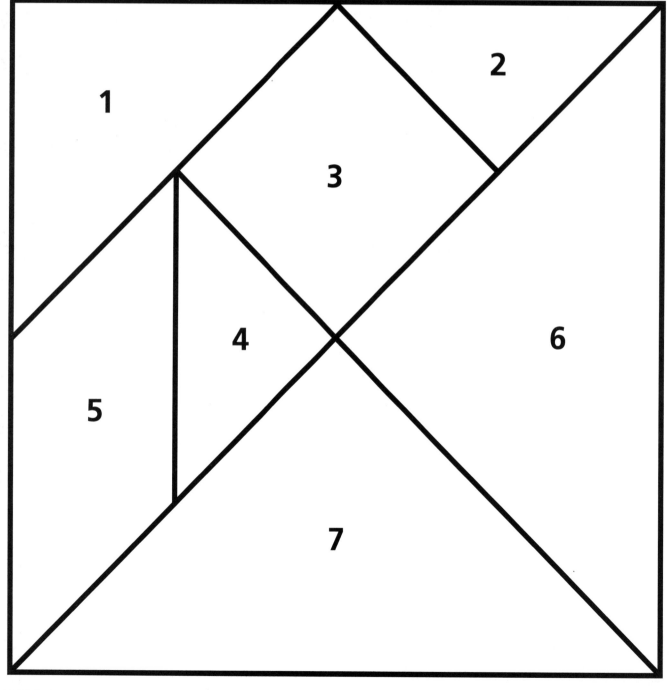

reproducible

MATH
Visual-Spatial Intelligence

Draw a Bigger Dragon

Using the letters and numbers on the grid, locate one square on the small grid, and then the same square on the large grid. Then copy the line in the square in the small grid to the larger grid.

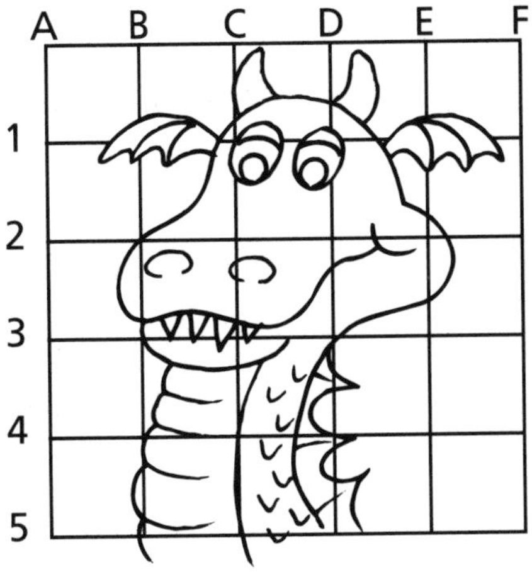

MATH

Visual-Spatial Intelligence

Three-D Magic

Use a pink highlighter to trace and color the stars, and a blue highlighter to trace the lines and outline the stars. When you have finished drawing, close your left eye and look at the drawing through the red plastic with your right eye. Then close your right eye and look at the drawing through the blue plastic piece. Finally, look through both eyes with the red plastic over the right eye, and the blue plastic over the left eye. Magic!

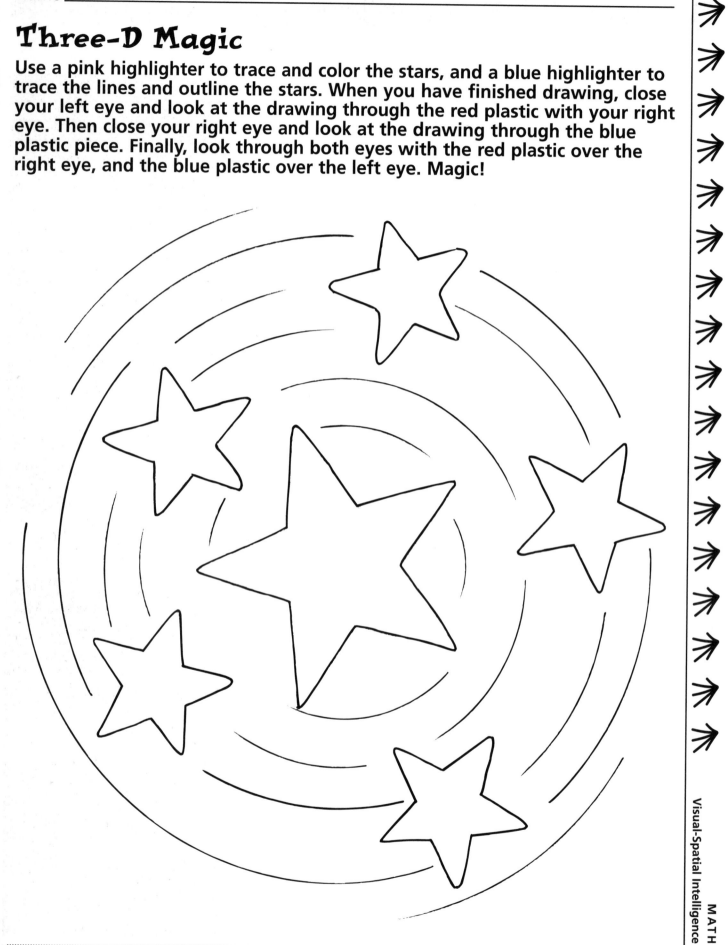

reproducible

MATH

Visual-Spatial Intelligence

Verbal-Linguistic Intelligence

Science Adjectives

In this activity students choose a science word, such as *clouds,* as in the example below. To each letter of the word students assign an adjective. The adjective, which starts with that letter, describes the science word. The activity can be extended by making mobiles out of the word collections.

Changing

Light

Overhead

Up

Dark

Soft

Blackout!

Discuss electricity and its importance in our lives. Consider such questions as: What things in the house or at school don't work without electricity? What would it feel like to lose electricity just as it is getting dark? How are pets affected? Do you think that having all the power off can make people act differently?

Tell students that in November 1965 in the evening all the electricity went off in the states of New York, Vermont, New Hampshire, Massachusetts, Connecticut, Rhode Island, and parts of Ontario, Canada. Explain that 30 million people were without electricity for 13 hours.

Have students write an essay about how they would react to a blackout.

Create a Science Picture Book

Show students some picture books of science topics, such as *Follow the Water from Brook to Ocean,* by Arthur Dorros (HarperCollins, 1991), *Tell Me a Season,* by Mary McKenna Siddals (Clarion, 1997), or *African Animals,* by Caroline Arnold (Morrow, 1997). Have students make their own simple science picture books about topics they are studying. They can illustrate the books themselves or use pictures found in magazines.

page 55

The Wind

This choral activity can be used with a weather unit. Pass out one copy to each student of the **A Poem** worksheet, found on page 55. The poem is "The Wind," by Robert Louis Stevenson. Tell the students that you will be doing a choral reading. Break up the class into three groups. Each group should read one of the verses. The entire class should read the refrain.

Five Senses Poem

Here is a closing linguistic intelligence activity to do with your class when you have finished studying the five senses. Have your students write a poem about a concrete object. Write the following format on the board for students to follow:

Line 1: _____ looks _____
Line 2: _____ sounds _____
Line 3: _____ smells _____
Line 4: _____ tastes _____
Line 5: _____ feels _____
Line 6: _____ is (are) _____

Give each student a sheet of writing paper. Tell them to choose a concrete object to write about. Then have the students draw a picture to accompany their poem. Let them share their beautiful accomplishments with the class.

Logical-Mathematical Intelligence

Magnet Fun

For this hands-on activity, give each student a bar or horseshoe magnet, a sheet of paper, and a pencil. Let the students investigate with their magnets to see which objects the magnet will and will not attract. Have the students keep two lists of these items on the sheet of paper. Then transfer their lists to the chalkboard. Extend the activity by giving questions, such as these: Can you make something jump to the magnet? What happens if you put your magnet next to another magnet? Does one end or section of a magnet attract items more strongly than another section? How could you test if your magnet is stronger or weaker than another magnet? Encourage students to write, illustrate, or explain their answers. Follow-up with the **Magnet Fun** worksheet on page 56.

page 56

Bodily-Kinesthetic Intelligence

Terrarium

Students can construct terrariums out of two plastic two-liter soda containers. Remove the labels from the bottles. Cut the top two-thirds off one bottle and the top half off the second. Poke 8 to 12 air holes in the half-bottle and make three 1-inch vertical slits at the rim so that it will slide into the 1/3 bottle. Cut a door in the side of the half-bottle that can be opened and easily resealed.

Place a layer of sand or gravel in the bottom. Then add soil and a bit of gardener's charcoal. Add a few small local plants and insects if desired. Water the soil well. Slide the top onto the base.

Observe the terrarium over a period of time and take notes in an observation log. Discuss what students have learned about their plants and animals in the project.

A Butterfly Pantomime

Let students move their bodies to learn the life stages of a butterfly. Begin by telling the students to think of themselves as a tiny egg on a leaf. Then ask them to listen to this narration and pantomime each step:

1. It's a warm summer day. You hatch from your egg and emerge as a larva, a tiny caterpillar. You crawl around eating leaves. You keep eating and eating green plants.

2. You have grown bigger and bigger until you've reached your full size as a caterpillar. You get ready to become a pupa. You attach yourself to a twig with a sticky liquid from your body. A hard shell, called a chrysalis, forms around you.

3. It is now winter. It's cold outside, but you are nice and cozy in your chrysalis.

4. Soon the weather starts to get warmer. It is spring. You can feel the sun shining. You have become an adult. Your shell cracks, and you emerge as a beautiful butterfly.

5. You fly around, stopping to drink nectar from flowers. In the summer, you lay tiny eggs on a leaf.

Weather Riddle Cards

Weather riddle cards may be used to introduce or reinforce vocabulary. You will need blank index cards, scissors, and glue. On the left side of each card, write a weather riddle. Example:

I am made by warm air rising, cooling, and condensing.

Then, on the right side of each card, write the corresponding vocabulary word. For example, *cloud*. Leave space between the riddle and vocabulary word. Now cut the cards into two parts, separating the riddle from the vocabulary word by using a wavy line. Place these cards in an envelope that has been decorated with weather symbols. Put the envelope at a center. Let students match up the riddles and terms. This card activity can be adapted to various topics across the curriculum. You may wish to have students make their own sets.

Visual-Spatial Intelligence

Tide Pool Concentration

This fun, challenging game encourages students to use their spatial intelligence while reviewing what they have learned about a tide pool. (You can adapt the idea to match any unit of study.) To make the game, you will need 16 index cards. Write each sea creatures' name on one card and its description on a separate card. If desired, include drawings or pictures of the animals on the name cards.

Let small groups play. Have them spread out the cards face down. Players take turns picking two cards and reading them aloud. If they match, the player keeps them and takes another turn. If they do not match, the player returns them. Play until all cards are matched. The player with the most pairs wins.

Text for Tide Pool cards:

Sand dollar—My flat round body has a star pattern on top. If you turn me over, I have a small hole in the center. This is my mouth.

Sea urchin—My body is ball-shaped and covered with long spines. I eat mostly plants found on rocks or the sea floor. My mouth is underneath my body. I have sharp teeth.

Sea star—I look like a star. My arms help me catch food. If I lose an arm, I can grow it back.

Sea anemone—When I open my tentacles, I look like a flower. With my tentacles, I catch little plants and animals that float by.

Mussel—I have two hard shells that are held together with a hinge. I attach myself to rocks on the ocean floor. When the tide comes in, I open and feed on tiny plants and animals floating in the water.

Hermit crab—I find an empty snail shell to live in. I have big, sharp claws and a soft belly.

Barnacle—I am a small shelled animal. I cement myself to a rock. When the tide comes in, I stick my feet out and catch something to eat.

Periwinkle—I am a small snail covered with a shell. To eat, I scrape algae off rocks.

Grid and Investigate

Read *Sunken Treasure*, by Gail Gibbons (HarperCollins, 1988). Discuss how grids help archaeologists and other scientists study a specific area.

Assign each student a square foot of ground to investigate. In each corner of the square students put a stake and run string around the perimeter. Have students draw what they see on a piece of paper of the same dimensions.

When students have finished their observation, the drawings can be displayed on the classroom wall to create a grid, with each grid square represented by a piece of paper.

Shadow Shapes

Mold four shapes out of modeling clay: a cube, a tetrahedron, a sphere, and a cylinder. Poke a piece of wire or a pencil into each shape so that it can be rotated without touching the sides. Using an overhead projector, have students do the following:

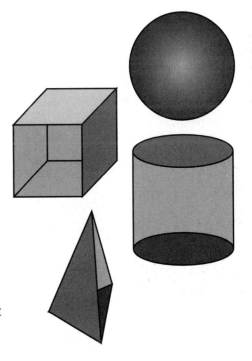

· Make the shadow of the tetrahedron look triangular.

· Make the shadow of the cube look square.

· Make the shadow of the sphere look circular.

· Make the shadow of the cylinder look rectangular, then circular.

Extend the activity by putting objects on the overhead projector and having students guess what they are. Hide the projector surface so that the students cannot see what is being projected.

Students can also make two- and three-dimensional shapes with wire. Have them experiment with making shadows from their shapes to discover which look three-dimensional when projected and why. Then they can explore what happens to the shadow when they alter the three-dimensional shape by detaching one of the sides.

Musical Intelligence

A Little Water Music

In this activity you will demonstrate the musical properties of water to your students. Collect a variety of drinking glasses, glass jars, and individual soda containers (plastic or glass). Fill a glass with water, wet a finger, and run it around the rim of the glass. A harmonic sound is created. Then change the water level and demonstrate again. A different pitch is created. Next, partially fill a soda container with water. Blow across the top of the bottle and show how music is made that way.

Divide students into groups. Let them experiment with the sounds made by combinations of glasses and soda bottles and different levels of water by tapping the containers with a spoon. Have groups make musical compositions with the water containers. Once students find a tone they like, they mark the water level on the glass with fingernail polish or acrylic paint, and label the containers with a number (1, 2, 3, 4, 5). As they create a composition, they write down the pattern of sound, such as 1, 1, 2, 5, 4, 3, and 1. Students can critique the music compositions after an in-class performance.

Sound Charades

Brainstorm a list of animals, objects, or actions that make a sound, such as a doorbell, a violin, a donkey, the ocean, a clock, water from a tap, etc. Write each sound on a blank card. Shuffle the cards.

Divide students into two teams. The first player on one team picks a card. Teammates turn their backs to the player and have one minute to guess the sound on the card by the audio clues the first player makes. No words may be used, but sound can be created with the mouth, the body, or any helpful objects. After the sound is correctly guessed or a minute has passed, the second team takes a turn.

Interpersonal Intelligence

The Board Room

In this activity students design their own board games. Explain the difference between a linear board game—one with a beginning and an end, such as The Game of Life—and a circular one, such as Monopoly. Discuss the kinds of games the students like to play and why they like them.

Divide the students into teams. Each team designs and decorates its own game board, doing its own research, creating its own game materials, and deciding what game pieces to use. Questions they may want to consider include:

- How does a player win the game?
- How many players can play?
- Which player goes first?
- What does each player do when it is his or her turn?
- If a player answers a question correctly, what happens?
- If a player answers a question incorrectly, what happens?

Some science topics that can be used for the games are dinosaurs, colors in nature, seasons, fruit and vegetables, favorite pets, and natural disasters.

Dialogues about Living

Discuss the need for food, water, sunlight, and shelter that we have in common with other living things. Compare and contrast human systems for meeting these needs with systems in plants and animals. *If Anything Ever Goes Wrong at the Zoo*, by Mary Jean Hendrick (Harcourt, Brace, Jovanovich, 1993), is a picture book that takes an amusing look at how animals might get their needs met.

Have students write short dialogues between two characters comparing and contrasting the way they get water, food, sunshine, and shelter. Possible pairs include: human, primate; human, dog; human, plant; plant, cat; worm, human; fish, panda; and bat, lizard.

Students can make stick puppets to represent their characters. After rehearsing their dialogues, they can present their dramatizations to the class.

Intrapersonal Intelligence

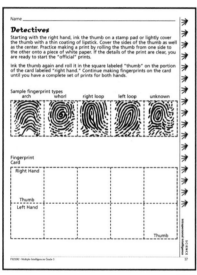

Natural Feelings

To learn a different mode of self-expression, students can compare how they feel to a natural phenomenon. Have students first get in touch with their feelings at present, and then recall some past emotions. Then they can assign a phenomenon in the natural world to these feelings. For example: *When I am angry, I feel like a volcano erupting. I get mad and let off smoke, and suddenly I'll explode!* Use these statements for a caption, and have students then draw a picture personifying the natural phenomena as themselves.

Detectives

Have the class take and analyze fingerprints using the **Detectives** worksheet found on page 57. The best materials for "inking" fingers are an inked stamp pad or lipstick. Starting with the right hand, ink the thumb on a stamp pad or lightly cover the thumb with a thin coating of lipstick. Cover the sides of the thumb as well as the flat part.

Practice making the prints before using the card. To make a print, roll the thumb from one side to the other on a piece of white paper. If the details of the print are clear, the student is ready to start the "official" prints. Have students make a complete set of prints for both hands. If a sink is not close at hand, baby wipes are good for cleaning fingertips.

Students can then compare their fingerprints to the print types shown in the the worksheet and decide what type of print each finger has: arch, whorl, right loop, or left loop. Sometimes arches and whorls look a lot alike. If there is no consensus on a particular print, mark it unknown (U). Use the first letter of each print type under each print to designate its type. Encourage students to compare their prints to view exactly how unique their fingerprints are.

page 57

A Poem

The Wind

by Robert Louis Stevenson

I saw you toss the kites on high

And blow the birds about the sky;

And all around I heard you pass,

Like ladies' skirts across the grass—

    O wind, a-blowing all day long,

    O wind, that sings so loud a song!

I saw the different things you did,

But always you yourself you hid.

I felt you push, I heard you call,

I could not see yourself at all—

    O wind, a-blowing all day long,

    O wind, that sings so loud a song!

O you that are so strong and cold,

O blower, are you young
or old?

Are you a beast of field and tree,

Or just a stronger child than me?

    O wind, a-blowing all day long,

    O wind, that sings so loud a song!

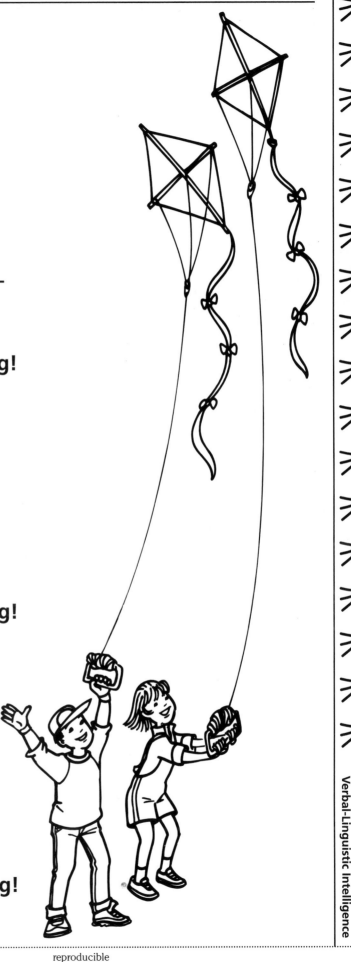

SCIENCE   Verbal-Linguistic Intelligence

Magnet Fun

Use the clues and the words in the Word Box to complete the puzzle.

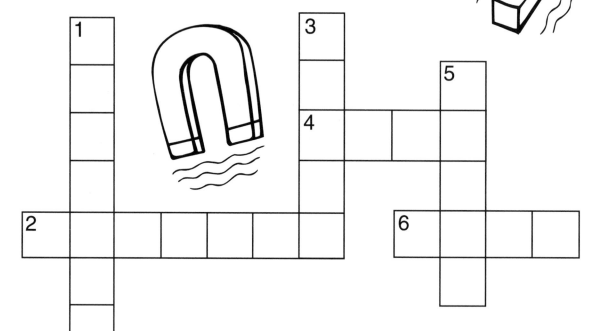

Word Box

lose	keep	attract
repel	magnets	poles

Down

1. Opposite poles _____, or draw toward each other.

3. Bar magnets have two _____, one on each end.

5. Like poles push away from each other, or _____.

Across

2. _____ are objects that can attract other objects.

4. Temporary magnets _____ their magnetism.

6. Permanent magnets _____ their magnetism.

SCIENCE   Logical-Mathematical Intelligence

Detectives

Starting with the right hand, ink the thumb on a stamp pad or lightly cover the thumb with a thin coating of lipstick. Cover the sides of the thumb as well as the center. Practice making a print by rolling the thumb from one side to the other onto a piece of white paper. If the details of the print are clear, you are ready to start the "official" prints.

Ink the thumb again and roll it in the square labeled "thumb" on the portion of the card labeled "right hand." Continue making fingerprints on the card until you have a complete set of prints for both hands.

Sample fingerprint types

arch	whorl	right loop	left loop	unknown

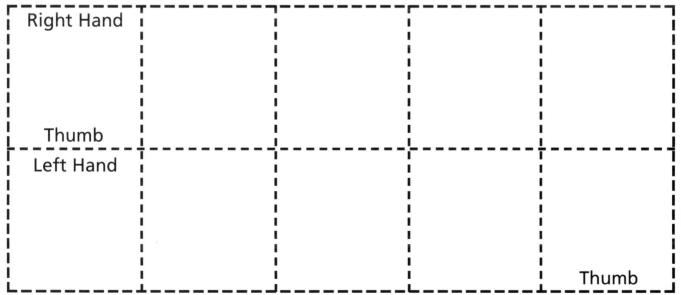

Fingerprint Card

Right Hand

Thumb

Left Hand

Thumb

SCIENCE
Intrapersonal Intelligence

Verbal-Linguistic Intelligence

Name Clouds

This activity is a good way for the class to learn students' names at the beginning of the school year. Provide each student with a large sheet of butcher paper. Instruct students to fold the paper in half. They should write their names in cursive handwriting to fill up most of the folded paper. Then they draw an outline around the outside of the letters, and then an outline around the outline to create an easy cut line. Use crayons, markers, or paint to decorate.

Next cut around the name, staple the top, sides, and part of the bottom. Stuff with wadded-up recyclable paper, then finish stapling the bottom. Attach yarn or cord and hang the name clouds above each child's desk.

Logical-Mathematical Intelligence

The Sierpinski Triangle

Before creating the Sierpinski Triangle, explain to your students that it is a famous fractal. A fractal is a geometric figure, such as a triangle, that is repeated many times to make a figure that is a more complex design.

Provide copies of the **Triangle Grid** worksheet found on page 65. Choose one triangle on the grid paper near the top of the paper toward the center of the grid. Color it. Then color in the triangle at the bottom left corner of the first colored triangle, and color in the triangle at the bottom right corner of the first colored triangle. Your figure will look like the

page 65

equilateral triangle below, with a side length of two triangle units and a blank triangle in the middle. It is your basic figure.

Next, at the bottom left corner of the basic figure, re-create the same triangle, with sides of two units and a blank triangle in the middle. Do the same at the bottom right corner of the basic figure. This is the second figure, seen below.

Finally, at the bottom left corner of the second figure, re-create the same triangle, with sides of 4 units and a blank triangle in the middle. Do the same at the bottom right corner of the second figure. Your pattern should now look like the third design at right. One large, three medium, and nine small triangles will be shaded. This is the Sierpinski Triangle.

The triangle can be enlarged on poster board and colored with a variety of colors to create patterns. A mural can be created if all student triangles are joined to form one huge Sierpinski Triangle.

Bodily-Kinesthetic Intelligence

Gesture Drawing

Explain to the class that gesture drawing is a drawing technique using quickly drawn lines that create a sense of energy and motion. The object of the exercise is to draw as fast as possible to capture the energy of the subject. Each drawing is created in 60 seconds, and the pen should be moving continually within this time period, without leaving the paper.

Gesture Drawing Directions

Materials: Construction paper, pen

1. Choose a volunteer to stand where she or he can be see by everyone in the class. The volunteer should strike a pose that conveys action, such as running, dancing, pitching a baseball, etc.

2. Have the students quickly draw the overall shape of the person. Their pens should never leave the paper as they draw. They are trying to draw an outline rather than capture details such as facial features, fingers, or hair.

3. Tell the students to start drawing faster. And even faster!

4. After one minute, their drawings are complete. Begin the procedure with a different model.

Visual-Spatial Intelligence

page 66

Showing Close and Far

Take students outside where they can look into the distance. Point out a tree or a house or other large object far away, and ask students to close one eye and use their fingers to show how big the object looks. Then do the same with another large object that is much closer to them. Discuss that the object farther away is not really smaller, it just looks smaller. Artists draw things small if they want them to look far away, and big if they want them to look close.

Using the **Close and Far** worksheet on page 66, students cut out the cacti and glue them into the desert scene to show how size and placement produce the illusion of space. Students should glue the large cactus near the bottom of the paper, in the foreground, and the smaller ones close to the top of the hill.

Musical Intelligence

Listening to Instruments

Invite students to listen to a recording of Prokofiev's *Peter and the Wolf* to study various musical instruments and the sounds they make. The words to the story are spoken with musical accompaniment, making the piece accessible to young listeners. And the instruments used to represent various characters are easy to pick out. A flute captures the twittering of a bird. The slinking of the cat is depicted by a clarinet. The low, sad sound of the oboe is the duck, and Peter's grandfather speaks in the grumbling tones of the bassoon. Challenge students to name the instruments that represent each character.

Classroom Environment

Recent research shows that there is a direct link between music and spatial reasoning. Called "the Mozart Effect," it has been demonstrated that listening to only ten minutes of Mozart's music improves performance in tasks requiring spatial intelligence. The master's music has also been shown to calm listeners and help them express themselves more clearly. In a study at the Center for Neurobiology of Learning and Memory at the University of California at Irvine, students scored eight to nine points higher on a spatial IQ test after listening to part of Mozart's "Sonata for Two Pianos in D Major."

Scientist believe the music helps organize the neuron firing patterns and strengthen the right-brain processes associated with spatial-temporal reasoning.

Before the class begins to work on an art project, let them listen to the CD *Mozart's Magic Fantasy,* by Susan Hammond (Children's Group, 1990), which takes students on a trip through Mozart's opera "The Magic Flute." Then play them some Mozart music as they create.

Interpersonal Intelligence

Color Wheel Mosaic

This art project will give students an opportunity to see the relationship of one color to another as they are positioned on a color wheel. In groups, students will create a mural-sized mosaic of the color wheel. Each student will be assigned a color and will create this portion of the mosaic.

Begin by displaying a large color wheel. Point out the primary colors—yellow, red, and blue—and secondary colors—orange, purple, and green. Explain that between these six colors are intermediate colors—yellow-orange, red-orange, red-violet, blue-violet, blue-green, and yellow-green. Complementary colors are colors that are found directly opposite each other on the wheel. Pairs of complementary colors are red and green, for example, and orange and blue.

Distribute **The Color Wheel** worksheet on page 67 to the class and have them color or paint the wheel with appropriate colors, trying to blend the colors together.

Before starting the project below, review the process of creating a mosaic with the class. Explain that historically mosaics were made with tile, stone, or glass pieces called tesserae. Display pictures of mosaics found in mosques, walls, or furniture. Jewelry and tile floors are also created with the mosaic technique.

Directions for a Color Wheel Mosaic

Materials: paper, watercolor or tempera paint or crayons, glue, scissors, glitter glue (optional)

1. Draw a large circle on butcher paper. On the inside of the circle mark lightly with pencil the 12 sections of the color wheel. Put the color wheel on a table where it is accessible. (More than one color wheel may be necessary depending on the number of students in the class.)

2. Each student should choose a primary or secondary color of the wheel.

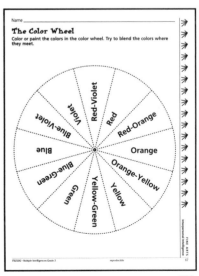

page 67

3. On white paper, students should draw a triangle the same size as a section of the color wheel. The paper should be colored with either crayons or paint before it is cut into small pieces. Each student will be creating a piece of the wheel, making sure that his or her color blends with the colors bordering it. Therefore, more than one color will be used by each student. For example, a student who chooses the color green will color his or her section green to yellow-green on one side, and green to blue-green on the other side.

4. Once the paper has been colored, it should be cut into small pieces.

5. Students can be working simultaneously to glue their tesserae to the wheel. Point out to students that they must leave room for other students to intersperse their tesserae around the borders of their colors so that the colors will blend nicely.

6. Glitter can be added to the finished spectrum.

7. Mount the color wheel on a wall when completed. The primary and secondary colors can be labeled.

8. Critique the finished artwork and discuss what worked well and what could be improved, what the students enjoyed about the project, and how they could apply the technique to other designs.

Extension Activities: Mosaics can be made with natural tesserae, such as seeds, beans, stones, and wood, attached to tagboard. Other materials that can be used are mirrors, foil, tissue, and a variety of papers. Mosaics can also be made with vinyl and linoleum tesserae on a Masonite board using grout as a filler.

Reference Materials: Books with examples of mosaics are *Piece by Piece! Mosaics of the Ancient World,* by Avi Avi-Yonah (Lerner, 1993), and *Whales,* by Lesley DuTemple (Lerner, 1996).

Drama in the Classroom

Encourage interested students to work in groups and present short plays to their classmates. Presentations can be as simple as a dramatic reading of the parts. Students can also stage their plays as full-scale productions with costumes, sets, and props. Check your school and community library for published plays. The library may also subscribe to *Plays: The Drama Magazine for Young People.* The magazine is published monthly from October through May. Each issue contains scripts suitable for middle and lower grade students. Skits and puppet shows are also featured. For subscription membership, contact Plays, Inc., 120 Boylston Street, Boston, MA 02116-4615.

Intrapersonal Intelligence

Dream Time

In this activity children will recall their dreams and write about them or create a picture of them. To set the mood for the project, read one or more of the following picture books about dreams: *Under the Moon*, by Dyan Sheldon (Dial, 1994), *Dream Meadow*, by Helen V. Griffith (Greenwillow, 1994), or *Plunk's Dreams*, by Helen V. Griffith (Greenwillow, 1990). Music and soft lighting can help create an environment to help the children recall their dreams. A relaxation exercise in which children lie on their backs (under trees if possible) can also put them in the proper state. If students are having difficulty remembering dreams, they can write or make a picture about one of their earliest memories. Allow them to use whatever medium they prefer to express themselves—poetry, short story, finger painting, colored pencils, etc.

Artists' Autobiographies

Read aloud *A Very Young Musician*, by Jill Krementz (Simon and Schuster, 1991). Or make the book available to interested students to read independently. This nonfiction book features a ten-year-old trumpet player. He describes how he got started, his lessons, practice sessions, and experiences that helped build his interest in music. Another biography is *A Young Painter*, by Zheng Zhensun and Alice Low (Scholastic, 1991), which is about a gifted young painter in China.

Invite interested students to create their own artistic autobiographies. Explain that they are not limited to music or painting—their art may be drama, voice, dance, drawing, sculpture, handicrafts, and so on. Encourage students to include photographs of themselves performing and practicing their art or illustrated examples of work they have created.

Naturalist Intelligence

Crayon Resist Art Project

This project helps students appreciate water in the world around them, and as a medium with which to create. Explain that they will be studying the interaction of water and wax in a process called crayon resist. In this technique crayon is applied to paper and then covered with watercolor. The

wax in the crayon will repel the water, so that the paint will not cover the crayon.

As a subject matter students should choose an image with water as its theme. Some suggestions are: a rainbow, an undersea picture, a surfer at the ocean, an aquarium, seashells on the shore.

Directions for Crayon Resist project

Materials: Construction paper, crayons, watercolors, paintbrushes, pencils

1. With a pencil, lightly sketch your picture on a sheet of white construction paper.

2. Use light-colored crayons to trace the pencil marks. Press firmly with the crayon.

3. Paint over the crayon areas with watercolor using broad horizontal strokes. Make sure to load your brush with lots of watercolor to make the painting bright.

Note: Be sure to show the class how to rinse the brush with water before using a new color.

Triangle Grid

Follow your teacher's directions for creating the Sierpinski Triangle.

FINE ARTS   Logical-Mathematical Intelligence

reproducible

Close and Far

Cut out the five saguaro cacti and place them in the desert scene to create the illusion of space and distance. Add any other details you like.

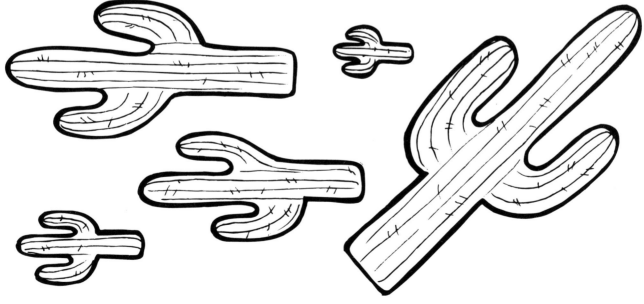

reproducible

FINE ARTS

Visual-Spatial Intelligence

The Color Wheel

Color or paint the colors in the color wheel. Try to blend the colors where they meet.

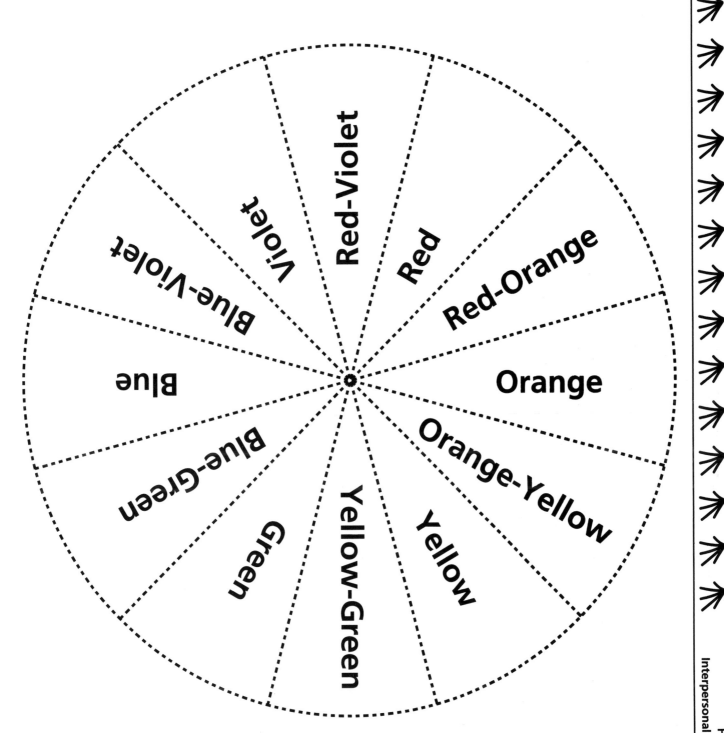

Verbal-Linguistic Intelligence

Lions and Tigers and Bears, Oh My!

Invite your students to brainstorm the names of professional sports teams. Record the names on chart paper and highlight those that involve animals. Then ask each student to select a team that has an animal name and have the student state why he or she thinks the team is named after that animal. Next, challenge the students to use encyclopedias, magazines, and sports books to discover the reasoning behind the team's name. Allow the student to present the information to the class. Finally, have each student create a name for a sports team and write a paragraph explaining why he or she chose the name.

Logical-Mathematical Intelligence

Change the Rules

Choose a playground game that your students enjoy, such as four square, tetherball, or kickball. Discuss with your students the rules of the chosen game. Then lead a brainstorming session in which new rules for the game are discussed. Have students select three to five of the new rules and make diagrams showing how the game would change if the new rules were implemented. Divide your students into teams and challenge them to follow the new rules for the game in a classroom tournament.

Count It Up!

Have each student track his or her progress in physical fitness for one month. Give your students copies of the **Count It Up!** worksheet found on page 73. Several times a week, have each student count the number of push-ups, stomach crunches, and jumping jacks he or she can complete. The student can log the information on his or her worksheet. At the end of the month, have the students create bar and line graphs for each activity using

page 73

the information from their worksheets.

Place Value Dribbling

Have each student work with a partner. Give each pair a basketball and allow the students time to practice dribbling the ball. Then tell the students they will change the way they dribble based on a number you call out. Assign an action for each place value in a three-digit number. For example, a spin can be the action for the hundreds place, a leg swing over the ball for the tens place, and a bounce between the legs for the ones place. Call out a number such as 352. Each student with a ball should begin dribbling and complete three spins (300), five leg swings over the ball (50) and two bounces between the legs (2).

Have the students practice this concept several times, allowing partners to take turns performing each number you call out in dribble movements. Then allow each pair to make up their own actions for each place value. The partners may take turns choosing the numbers and dribbling the ball.

Bodily-Kinesthetic Intelligence

Animal Relays

Designate a starting line and a finish line of the relay. Then divide the class into groups of four. Have each group sit single-file behind the starting line. Explain to the students that they will imitate the movements of animals in this relay. Ask a volunteer to name an animal and have him or her demonstrate a movement for that animal. For example, to move like a kangaroo, the student may hop forward with both feet together. The first student in each line will move from the starting line to the finish line and back to the starting line in the same way that was demonstrated. When the students return to the starting line, they will go to the ends of their lines and the next student in each line will perform the same task. After each group has completed the relay, call on another volunteer to demonstrate a new animal movement for the groups to perform.

Visual-Spatial Intelligence

Perfect Playground

Talk with your students about the school playground. Encourage them to point out the qualities of the playground they enjoy as well as the areas they feel need improvement. Then discuss the issues that go into planning a playground, such as safety, equipment, use of space, and so on. Divide the students into groups and challenge each group to design a "perfect playground." Provide each group with graph paper to sketch out the initial design. Then give each group a sheet of heavy cardboard and various art materials (construction paper, scissors, glue, markers, etc.) to build a model of its playground. Allow each group to present its model to the class.

Pop-Ups

Take a photograph of each student participating in a sport. After the film is developed, help the students to make a pop-up card featuring their photographs. Give each student two sheets of colored construction paper and have him or her follow these directions to make the card:

1. Fold one sheet of construction paper in half.

2. Cut two half-inch slits from the fold near the center of the paper to make a tab. See illustration at left.

3. Unfold the paper and push out the tab.

4. Fold the second sheet of paper in half and glue it to the back of the first sheet. Make sure you do not glue down the tab.

5. Write a special message in your card and decorate the front and inside.

6. Cut around your photograph so that only your image is left.

7. Glue your image to the tab and deliver your card to a family member or friend.

Musical Intelligence

Freeze Dance

Have the students spread out over a large area. Play some music and encourage students to dance. Periodically, stop the music. When the music stops, the students must freeze. Call out the names of any students who are seen moving. Those students will then move to the side of the playing area and will help judge whether or not other students move. Begin the music again, and tell the remaining students to resume dancing. Repeat the process until only a few students are left in the playing area.

Balloon Body Bounce

Give each student an inflated balloon and choose one student to be the leader. The leader may select a song to play and then call out directions for bouncing the balloons off the body. For example, the leader might instruct the students to bounce the balloons on their hands, then their heads, knees, hips, and so on. A new leader should be chosen at the end of the song.

Interpersonal Intelligence

Group Seating

This event requires trust and working together. Have the students stand in a circle shoulder to shoulder. Tell them to make a quarter turn to the right and take a step sideways into the circle. Then tell them to bend their knees and sit. If everyone works together, each student will be sitting on another student's knees in the circle. If one person falls, all will fall. When the students can do this successfully, encourage them to make a "wave" with their arms, one student raising and lowering both arms at a time.

Coaching

Hold a discussion about the role of coaches in sports. Talk about the importance of a coach's ability to communicate clearly and positively. Have students suggest ideas they have for positive comments.

Select a skill to practice, such as kicking a ball, dribbling a ball, or hitting a ball with the palm of the hand. Have pairs of students take turns acting as coach and athlete. The athlete will practice the skill as the coach will practice offering suggestions and positive comments. Follow up the activity with a discussion about the coaching methods that were helpful and those that were not helpful.

Intrapersonal Intelligence

Interest Inventory

Give each student a copy of the **Interest Inventory** worksheet found on page 74. Have the students complete the inventories independently. Then, on the back of the paper, have each student write three physical fitness goals he or she has. Encourage the student to describe ways in which the goals may be achieved. Collect the inventories and keep them in student portfolios. Later they can be re-evaluated by the students and discussed at parent-teacher conferences.

page 74

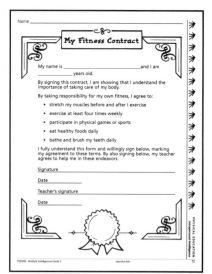

page 75

Fitness Contract

Encourage each student in your class to take responsibility for his or her health and fitness. Hold a class discussion about the importance of exercise, nutrition, and personal hygiene. Then invite your students to read and sign a copy of the **My Fitness Contract** found on page 75. Tell your students that by signing the contract, they are making a commitment to themselves to exercise regularly, to eat well-balanced meals, and to attend to their personal cleanliness.

Naturalist Intelligence

Nature Walk

Take your students on a nature walk around the community. Have the students collect different kinds of leaves, rocks, feathers, and other natural objects. Have them keep notes of where each item was found. Once back at school, have each student draw a map of the walk. Have the student glue or tape each item that was collected to the map, in the general area where it was found.

Outdoors Project

Students can create a personal project based on an outdoor activity that they enjoy doing on their own. Some activities to choose from are: hiking, fishing, camping, bird watching, cross-country skiing, running. Have the students create a list of goals they'd like to meet in this activity. (Parental supervision will be needed for some activities.) Students can also include any of the following in their project: safety tips for the sport or activity, instructions on how to perform a task or skill related to the activity, a map, a photo essay, or a journal. Have students present their reports to the class.

Name _____

Count It Up!

Count the number of push-ups, stomach crunches, and jumping jacks you can complete. Record the information on the chart.

Date	Push-ups	Stomach crunches	Jumping Jacks

Interest Inventory

1. Do you like to play sports or do you prefer to watch them? Use the space below and on the back of the paper to write about your feelings.

   _____

   _____

2. List any sports you participate in after school or on the weekends.

   _____

   _____

3. List some sports that you might like to learn about.

   _____

   _____

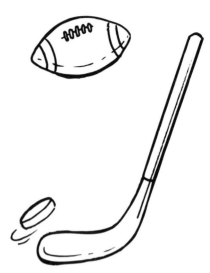

4. Circle a number from 1 to 5 to describe your skill level for each activity below.

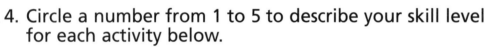

throwing a ball

1	2	3	4	5
not so well		okay		very well

catching a ball

1	2	3	4	5
not so well		okay		very well

bouncing a ball

1	2	3	4	5
not so well		okay		very well

kicking a ball

1	2	3	4	5
not so well		okay		very well

running

1	2	3	4	5
not so well		okay		very well

jumping

1	2	3	4	5
not so well		okay		very well

being a good sport

1	2	3	4	5
not so well		okay		very well

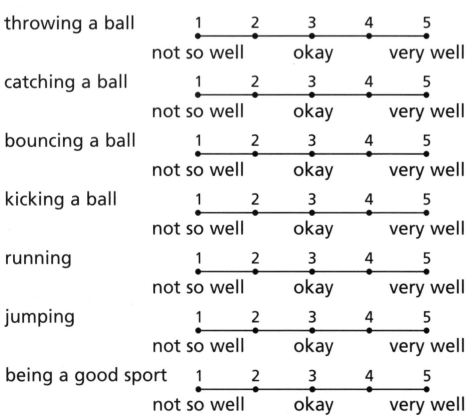

PHYSICAL EDUCATION
Intrapersonal Intelligence

reproducible FS23282 · Multiple Intelligences Grade 3

Name _____

My Fitness Contract

My name is _____ and I am

_____ years old.

By signing this contract, I am showing that I understand the importance of taking care of my body.

By taking responsibility for my own fitness, I agree to:

- stretch my muscles before and after I exercise

- exercise at least four times weekly

- participate in physical games or sports

- eat healthy foods daily

- bathe and brush my teeth daily

I fully understand this form and willingly sign below, marking my agreement to these terms. By also signing below, my teacher agrees to help me in these endeavors.

Signature _____

Date _____

Teacher's signature _____

Date _____

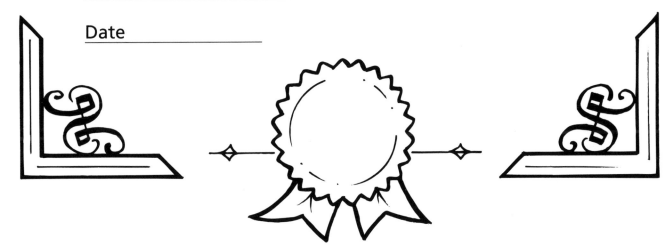

Page 37 Tangram Puzzle

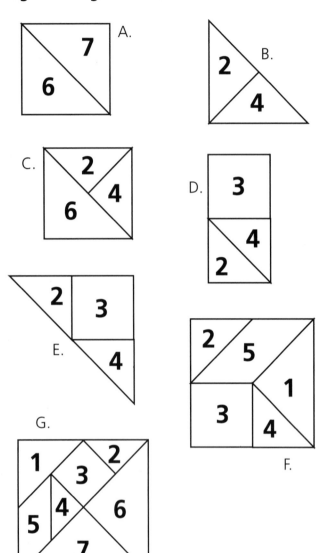

Page 56 Magnet Fun
DOWN: 1. attract 3. poles 5. repel
ACROSS: 2. magnets 4. lose 6. keep